TRANSLATION PROBLEMS
FROM A TO Z

SIL International®

Scripture quotations marked CEV are from the *Contemporary English Version*, copyright © 1991 by the American Bible Society.

Scripture quotations marked KJV are from the *King James Version*.

Scripture quotations marked ISV are from the Holy Bible, International Standard Version®. Copyright © 1998 by the Learn Foundation, Yorba Linda, CA. Used by permission of Davidson Press. All rights reserved internationally.

Scripture quotations marked LB are from the *Living Bible*, copyright © 1971 by Tyndale House Publishers.

Scripture quotations marked NCV are from The Holy Bible: New Century Version, copyright © 1997, 1988, 1991 by Word Publishing, Nashville, Tennessee 37214. Used by permission.

Scripture quotations marked NET are from The Holy Bible: The NET BIBLE® (New English Translation®). Copyright © 1998 by Biblical Studies Press, L.L.C. (www.netbible.org)

Scripture quotations marked NIV are from the *Holy Bible: New International Version*, copyright © 1973, 1978, 1984 by the International Bible Society, used by permission of Zondervan Bible Publishers.

Scripture quotations marked NLT are from the *Holy Bible*, New Living translation, copyright © 1996. Used by permission of Tyndale House Publishers, Inc., Wheaton, Illinois 60189.

Scripture quotations marked NRSV are from the *New Revised Standard Version Bible*, copyright © 1989 by the Division of Christian Education of the National Council of the Churches of Christ in the U.S.A.

Scripture quotations marked REB are from *The Revised English Bible*, copyright © 1989 by Oxford University Press and Cambridge University Press.

Scripture quotations marked TEV are from *Today's English Version*, copyright © 1966, 1971, 1976 by the American Bible Society, used by permission. (Also published as *Good News Bible*.)

Other translations are the author's own for the purpose of showing how a solution might be applied to a text.

The author has italicized some words in the Scripture quotations for the purpose of highlighting the words that are involved in a problem.

TRANSLATION PROBLEMS
A FROM TO Z

REVISED EDITION

Richard C. Blight

Summer Institute of Linguistics

© 1992, 1999 by SIL International®
Library of Congress Catalog No: 2017961174
ISBN: 978-1-55671-441-2

Printed in the United States of America

No part of this publication may be reproduced, stored in a retrieval system, or transmitted in any form or by any means—electronic, mechanical, photocopy, recording, or otherwise—without the express permission of SIL International®. However, short passages, generally understood to be within the limits of fair use, may be quoted without written permission.

Copies of this and other publications of SIL International® may be obtained through distributors such as Amazon, Barnes & Noble, other worldwide distributors and, for select volumes, www.sil.org/resources/publications:

SIL International Publications
7500 W. Camp Wisdom Road
Dallas, Texas 75236-5629 USA

General inquiry: publications_intl@sil.org
Pending order inquiry: sales_intl@sil.org
www.sil.org/resources/publications

This book was produced from a digitally scanned reproduction of the original publication.

Cover Design

Barbara Alber

CONTENTS

Alphabetical Listing of Categories 6
Topical Listing of Categories 7
Preface 9
Systematic Recording of Consultant Notes 83

ALPHABETICAL LISTING OF CATEGORIES

with their topical codes:

[Co] Communication
[Cu] Culture
[D] Discourse
[E] Exegesis and Text
[G] Grammar
[L] Lexicon
[Rh] Rhetoric and Highlighting
[RL] Receptor Language and Setting

Accuracy in translation [Co] 11
Ambiguity in translation [Co] 11
Anachronism [Cu] 12
Apostrophe [Rh] 12
Assumed information [Co] 13
Book introduction [RL] 14
Book title [RL] 15
Chiasmus [D] 15
Chronological order of events [D] . 16
Clarity in translation [Co] 18
Cohesion/transition [D] 18
Collocation [L] 19
Comparative relation [G] 20
Condition [G] 21
Connotation [L] 22
Cross-cultural mismatch [Cu] 22
Cross-reference [RL] 23
Cultural substitute (See Unknown idea)
Discourse unit [D] 23
Double meaning (author intended ambiguity) [E] 24
Doublet (See Parallelism)
Ellipsis [G] 25
Emotive focus [Co] 25
Euphemism [Rh] 26
Figurative extension [Rh] 27
Footnote [RL] 28
Form [Rh] 29
Formula [D] 30
Front and back matter [RL] 30
Genitive in source text [G] 31
Genre [D] 32
Glossary [RL] 33
Hendiadys [Rh] 34
Hyperbole [Rh] 35
Idiom [L] 35
Illocutionary force [Co] 36
Implicature [Co] 36
Influence [RL] 38
Information load [D] 39
Interpretation of source text [E] 39
Irony [Rh] 41
Key biblical term [L] 42
Layout in RL [RL] 42
Lexical correspondence [L] 42
Litotes [Rh] 45
Metaphor [Rh] 45
Metonymy (See Figurative extension)
Miscellaneous 47
Naturalness in translation [Co] 48
Negation [G] 48
Numbering [RL] 50
Old Testament quotation [E] 50
Omission of information in translation [Co] 52
Orthography issues [RL] 52
Other grammatical relationships (with in a clause or proposition) [G] ... 53
Parable and allegory [Rh] 53
Parallel passage [RL] 53
Parallelism [Rh] 54
Participant reference [D] 56
Passive voice [G] 57
Personification [Rh] 58
Perspective/direction [D] 59
Picture selection [RL] 60
Poetry [D] 60
Prominence [D] 62
Pronominal reference [G] 63
Proper name [L] 65
Relationship between propositions [D] 67
Relative clause [G] 68
Repetition [Rh] 68
Rhetorical question [Rh] 69
Section heading [RL] 70
Simile [Rh] 71
Skewing between grammar and semantics [G] 72
Sociolinguistic setting [Co] 73
Sound symbolism [Rh] 74
Speech quotation [D] 74
Symbolism [Cu] 75
Synecdoche (See Figurative extension)
Tense and aspect [G] 76
Textual variant [E] 77
Theme [D] 78
Unknown idea [Cu] 78
Vocative [Rh] 81
Zeugma [Rh] 82

TOPICAL LISTING OF CATEGORIES

DISCOURSE [D]
Chiasmus 15
Chronological order of events 16
Cohesion/transition 18
Discourse unit 23
Formula 30
Genre 32
Information load 39
Participant reference 56
Perspective/direction 59
Poetry 60
Prominence 62
Relationship between propositions 67
Speech quotation 74
Theme 78

EXEGESIS AND TEXT [E]
Double meaning (author intended ambiguity) 24
Interpretation of source text 39
Old Testament quotation 50
Textual variant 77

COMMUNICATION [Co]
Accuracy in translation 11
Ambiguity in translation 11
Assumed information 13
Clarity in translation 18
Emotive focus 25
Illocutionary force 36
Implicature 36
Naturalness in translation 48
Omission of information in translation 52
Sociolinguistic setting 73

GRAMMAR [G]
Comparative relation 20
Condition 21
Ellipsis 25
Genitive in source text 31
Negation 48
Other grammatical relationships (within a clause or proposition) . 53
Passive voice 57
Pronominal reference 63
Relative clause 68
Skewing between grammar and semantics 72
Tense and aspect 76

CULTURE [Cu]
Anachronism 12
Cross-cultural mismatch 22
Cultural substitute (See Unknown idea)
Symbolism 75
Unknown idea 78

LEXICON [L]
Collocation 19
Connotation 22
Idiom 35
Key biblical term 42
Lexical correspondence 42
Proper name 66

RHETORIC AND HIGHLIGHTING [Rh]
Apostrophe 12
Doublet (See Parallelism)
Euphemism 26
Figurative extension) [Rh] 27
Form [Rh] 29
Hendiadys 34
Hyperbole 35
Irony 41
Litotes 45
Metaphor 45

Metonymy (See Figurative extension)
Parable and allegory 53
Parallelism........................... 54
Personification 58
Repetition............................. 68
Rhetorical question................. 69
Simile................................... 71
Sound symbolism................... 74
Synecdoche (See Figurative extension)
Vocative............................... 81
Zeugma 82

RECEPTOR LANGUAGE AND SETTING [RL]
Book introduction................... 14
Book title............................. 15
Cross-reference 23
Footnote 28
Front and back matter............. 30
Glossary 33
Influence 38
Layout in receptor language...... 42
Numbering 50
Orthography issues 52
Parallel passage 53
Picture selection.................... 60
Section heading..................... 70

MISCELLANEOUS 47

PREFACE

Over six thousand languages are spoken in the world, all of them differing from one another in matters of lexical items, grammar, idioms, and figures of speech. Furthermore, the historical and cultural settings for the speakers of one language differ considerably from those for speakers of another language. It is not surprising that many problems are encountered in translating a message from one language to another. Here is a collection of the types of translation problems consultants find over and over again as they check translations of the Bible.

Problems

The Summer Institute of Linguistics and the United Bible Societies have worked together to develop a list of categories that translation consultants can refer to as they report on the problems they encounter while checking translations. By using a computer-based system of reporting, it is possible to retrieve all the examples of any particular category. Those looking for illustrative examples for teaching or research purposes will find this feature to be invaluable.

The description of each category has been adopted by the United Bible Societies and the Summer Institute of Linguistics. These categories are recognized in the UBS TRIDAT database of notes and in the SIL CONNOT (Consultant Notes) database of resource notes and in the Translator's Bible Index that will link Paratext and Translator's Workplace CD-ROM. The system of recording CONNOT notes is described at the end of this book.

A problem that has appeared in many languages is then given. Translators will not encounter all of the problems described in this book in any one language, but they are sure to encounter some of them. In addition to these widespread problems, every language will present some unique problems to be solved.

Solutions

When translators encounter a problem, they can look at the solutions suggested in this book to see how others have solved it. Then they need to consider how to best solve it in their own languages. Many times, the solutions suggested here will be one possible way, but there may be a better way tailored to their specific languages. Most of the solutions have an example found in one or more English versions.

Acknowledgments

John Beekman was the first International Translation Coordinator for the Summer Institute of Linguistics. He began collecting reports of the problems that he and the consultants working with him encountered. They described each problem on a separate slip of paper. As hundreds of these slips accumulated, they were sorted according to the types of problems they illustrated. These problems were analyzed and provided a basis for lectures at translation workshops and for articles in the periodical, *Notes on Translation* (Dallas: Summer Institute of Linguistics). The principles and guidelines that developed from this study were then described by John Beekman and John Callow in *Translating the Word of God* (Grand Rapids: Zondervan, 1974).

Ten years after John Beekman began his translation workshops, I wrote an article "Translation Problems from A to Z" (*Notes on Translation*, No. 46, 1972) in which I listed the types of problems that consultants had been encountering. Later I wrote a revised and expanded version, using the same name. Now, this book has again been revised and enlarged to agree with the wording of a committee composed of consultants of the United Bible Society and of the Summer Institute of Linguistics.

Consultants who have had experience in other parts of the world have reviewed the contents of this manual. I appreciate the helpful suggestions made by the following translation consultants: Jerry Allen (Solomon Islands and Papua New Guinea), Katharine Barnwell (International Translation Coordinator and former Africa Area Coordinator), Dick Hohulin (Philippines and Pacific Area), and Willis Ott (Sudan and Bolivia).

ACCURACY IN TRANSLATION —whether a given rendering in the receptor language accurately communicates the meaning of the original text.

Problem: The translation has not been tested to see how accurately it communicates.

Solution: Every translation needs to be tested extensively before it is printed. The use of comprehension testing questions is an important method by which translations can be tested. Carefully prepared questions enable a translator or consultant to discover how accurately a translation communicates the message of the original text. The questions and expected answers should be based on the meaning of the Greek text. Then if the answers to questions about the translation agree with the answers derived from the Greek text, we can be confident that the same message is being communicated. If an answer does not agree with a prepared answer, it should be determined whether it is because (1) a wrong meaning is being communicated in the translation, (2) the question has not been asked correctly, (3) the question has not been understood, or (4) the answer is not the same as most other readers would give.

AMBIGUITY IN TRANSLATION —whether a given rendering in the receptor language may allow the audience to understand a meaning that was not intended and which is not accurate to the author's intended meaning.
- 📖 Romans 1:17 (KJV) "For therein is *the righteousness of God* revealed from faith to faith." (Also ambiguous ISV, NET, NRSV, REB.)
- 📖 1 Timothy 5:3 (NCV) "Take care of widows *who are truly widows.*"

Problem: The translation can be taken in two ways. For example, in Romans some have taken "righteousness" to be an attribute of God, while most commentators take it to be a state of righteousness that God confers on sinners.

Solution: Translate so that the intended meaning is clearly communicated.
- 📖 Romans 1:17 (NIV) "For in the gospel a *righteousness from God* is revealed, a righteousness that is by faith from first to last."

(NLT) "This Good News tells us how *God makes us right in his sight*. This is accomplished from start to finish by faith." (Similarly CEV, NCV, TEV.)

📖 1 Timothy 5:3 (CEV) "Take care of any widow *who is really in need*." (Similarly NET, NIV.)
(NLT) "The church should care for any widow *who has no one else to care for her*."
(TEV) "Show respect for widows *who really are all alone*."

ANACHRONISM —something that is out of place in respect to the historical setting. It is anachronistic to refer to something in a translation that did not exist at the time of the original setting, or, if in existence, had not yet become known or used in that setting.

📖 Isaiah 60:11 (NLT) "Your gates will stay open *around the clock* to receive the wealth of many lands."

📖 Matthew 13:52 (LB) "Those experts in Jewish law who are now my disciples have double treasures—from the *Old Testament* as well as from the *New!*"

📖 Revelation 18:22 (LB) "Never again will the sound of music be there—no more *pianos, saxophones*, and trumpets."

Problem: The translation is not true to the historical setting.

Solution: Do not change the historical setting. Readers should understand that the Bible was written in another culture at a much earlier time. Sometimes the translator may decide that a slight anachronism in a cultural substitute is acceptable. For example, avocados might be substituted for figs if figs are unknown and the passage is used for teaching a point not dependent on the historical presence of the item.

📖 Matthew 7:16 "Are grapes gathered from thorns, or *avocados* [instead of *figs*] from thistles?"

Also, modern terms for weights and measures are more meaningful than transliterations for such things as *saton, talent, hin, omer*, and *beka*.

📖 Matthew 13:33 (TEV) "A woman takes some yeast and mixes it with a bushel [instead of *three satons*] of flour."

APOSTROPHE —inanimate or abstract ideas are addressed directly as if they were people. People who are not present are addressed directly.

- Matthew 2:6 (NRSV) "And *you*, Bethlehem, ... are by no means least."
- Romans 2:1 (NIV) "*You* [singular], therefore, have no excuse, *you* who pass judgment on someone else."
- 1 Corinthians 15:55 (NLT) "O death, where is your victory? O death, where is your sting?"

Problems: (1) The reader of the translation does not recognize that the expression is figurative and takes the statement literally. (2) The reader recognizes that the statement is not to be taken literally, but does not properly relate the figurative expression with its intended meaning.

Solution: Change from the second-person form to a third-person form.
- Matthew 2:6 "And Bethlehem ... is by no means least."
- Romans 2:1 "There is no excuse for *a person* who passes judgment on someone else."
- 1 Corinthians 15:54b–55 (CEV) "Death has lost the battle! Where is its victory? Where is its sting?"

ASSUMED INFORMATION

—the facts that the author of the original message expected the readers to know. Usually these facts are things that are culturally specific, or historical knowledge, or geographical locations. Information contained in the Old Testament is often assumed to be known to the original readers. Since such material was known to his readers, the author could leave implicit some points that are vital for understanding his message.
- Mark 1:6 (NIV) "John wore clothing made of camel's hair, with a leather belt around his waist."
- 1 Corinthians 10:1 (NRSV) "I do not want you to be unaware, brothers and sisters, that our ancestors were all under the cloud, and all passed through the sea."

Problem: The readers of a translation do not know all the facts known by the original readers and so do not understand all that the writer intended to communicate.

Solutions: Essential background information should be supplied so that new readers will be able to understand the author's message. There are various ways to provide such information.
  1. Some information vital to good understanding of the primary message can be included in the text if it can be fitted in easily without distorting the focus of the discourse.

ASSUMED INFORMATION

- 📖 Mark 1:9 (NCV) "At that time Jesus came from *the town of* Nazareth in Galilee and was baptized by John in the Jordan *River.*"
- 📖 1 Corinthians 10:1 (TEV) "I want you to remember, my brothers, what happened to our ancestors *who followed Moses.* They were all under *the protection of* the cloud, and all passed *safely* through the *Red* Sea."
  (NLT) "I don't want you to forget, dear brothers and sisters, what happened to our ancestors *in the wilderness long ago.* God guided all of them by sending a cloud *that moved along ahead of them*, and he brought them all safely through *the waters* of the sea *on dry ground.*"

2. Begin the book with a short introduction, which includes essential information for understanding the book as a whole.

3. Use footnotes to provide needed information for individual verses.
   - 📖 Mark 1:6 (TEV) John wore clothes made of camel's hair, with a leather belt around his waist." Footnote: "2 K 1.8."
     (NET) "John wore a garment made of camel's hair with a leather belt around his waist." Footnote: " . . . While his clothing and diet were indicative of someone who lived in the desert, they also depicted him in his role as God's prophet (cf. Zech 13:4); his appearance is similar to the Prophet Elijah (2 Kings 1:8)."

4. Provide a glossary to explain some of the words used in the translation, e.g., Pharisee, Passover, day of rest.

5. Include historically accurate pictures to show unknown objects, e.g., camel, bear, fig tree, grapevine, watchtower, a shepherd guarding his sheep, a man sowing seeds by scattering them.

6. Produce supplemental books to describe and illustrate biblical culture and history.

BOOK INTRODUCTION —information for an introduction to a particular book of the Bible. The information should be relevant and helpful for correctly understanding the book. It may describe who wrote the book, to whom it was written, the main theme of the book, and background information, such as the historical situation and additional cultural or historical information that the author assumes that the readers already know.

BOOK INTRODUCTION 15

Problem: The introduction has too much material or not enough.

Solution: The introduction should have information that is of importance to the whole, or major part, of the book. Information that is relevant to only one part of the book should be put in a footnote or glossary.

BOOK TITLE —any issue relating to the translation of the title of a Scripture volume (such as a Bible or New Testament) or of any individual Bible book title.

Problem: Titles have followed the grammar of other languages and are not meaningful in the receptor language.

Solution: Languages have their own ways of stating titles. Some may simply state the topic without using a verb. Others will require complete sentences. Some will need introductory phrase such as, "Here is . . . ," "Here it tells about . . . ," or "This is what . . ."

CHIASMUS —an arrangement of a series of statements in which there is a correspondence between the first and the last, between the second and the second to last, and so on. This is symbolized as ABBA, ABCCBA, using as many letters as there are levels of correspondence.
- Matthew 7:6 (KJV) "[A] Give not that which is holy unto the dogs, [B] neither cast ye your pearls before swine, [B] lest they trample them under their feet, [A] and turn again and rend you."
- Philemon 1:5 (ISV) "[A] For I hear about your love [B] and the faith that you have [B] toward the Lord Jesus [A] and for all the saints."

Problem: The reader misunderstands how the statements are related. For example, Matthew 7:6 might be understood to mean that the swine trample the pearls under their feet and also turn and tear the people to pieces (apparently it is taken this way by ISV, NET, NIV, NLT, NRSV, and REB). Philemon 1:2 might be understood to mean that Philemon had faith both in the Lord Jesus and in all the saints.

Solutions:
1. Rearrange the statements so that the reader will relate them correctly.
    - Matthew 7:6 (TEV) "[A] Do not give what is holy to dogs— [A] they will only turn and attack you. [B] Do not throw your pearls in front of pigs—[B] they will only trample them underfoot."

📖 Philemon 1:5 (TEV) "[A] For I hear of your love [A] for all of God's people [B] and the faith you have [B] in the Lord Jesus." (Similarly NCV, NRSV.)
(CEV) "[B] I hear about your faith [B] in our Lord Jesus [A] and about your love [A] for all of God's people." (Similarly NET, NIV, NLT.)

2. Make the participants explicit in each clause.
📖 Matthew 7:6 (NCV) "[A] Don't give holy things to dogs, [B] and don't throw your pearls before pigs. [B] *Pigs* will only trample on them, [A] and *dogs* will turn to attack you."

CHRONOLOGICAL ORDER OF EVENTS

—the sequence of events arranged in the order of the time of their occurrence. Events are commonly reported in the order in which they occurred, but sometimes they can be reported in a different order. Three types of sequence may cause problems.

1. *Non-historical order.* Events are reported in a sequence that does not match the historical order.
   📖 Luke 5:28 (KJV) "And he left all, rose up, and followed him."
   📖 Luke 10:34 (NIV) "He went to him and bandaged his wounds, pouring on oil and wine."

   Problem: The reported order of events confuses the reader about the actual historical order, or stands out as being an unusual way to list the events.

   Solution: If it is natural to relate the events in the order in which they happened, rearrange them so as to present the historical order.
   📖 Luke 5:28 (NRSV) "And he got up, left everything, and followed him." (Similarly NCV, NIV, NLT, TEV.)
   📖 Luke 10:34 (TEV) "He went over to him, poured oil and wine on his wounds and bandaged them," (Similarly CEV, NCV, NLT.) Or, probably even more exactly, "He went over to him, poured wine and then oil on his wounds, and bandaged them."

2. *Flashback.* An event which occurred prior to the sequence of events being described interrupts the strict chronological order of events.
   📖 John 4:7, 8, 9 "A Samaritan woman came to draw some water, and Jesus said to her, 'Please give me a drink.' For his disciples had gone off into town to buy food. The Samaritan woman said

to him, 'How can you, a Jew, ask for a drink from me, a Samaritan woman?'"

Problem: The flashback confuses readers when they do not understand how it relates to the rest of the narrative.

Solutions:
1. Use the way in which the language indicates such flashbacks. A receptor language might use verb signals, repeat clauses preceding the flashback at the end of the flashback, or treat the flashback as a parenthesis.

    📖 John 4:7, 8, 9 (TEV) "A Samaritan woman came to draw some water, and Jesus said to her, 'Give me a drink of water.' (His disciples had gone into town to buy food.) The woman answered, 'You are a Jew, and I am a Samaritan—so how can you ask me for a drink?'" (Similarly NCV, NET, NIV, NRSV.)

    (NLT) "Soon a Samaritan woman came to draw water, and Jesus said to her, 'Please give me a drink.' He was alone at the time because his disciples had gone into the village to buy some food. The woman was surprised, for Jews refuse to have anything to do with Samaritans. She said to Jesus, 'You are a Jew, and I am a Samaritan woman. Why are you asking me for a drink?'"

2. Reorder the events to show the actual order in which they happened. When reordering extends beyond one verse, it should only be done to avoid wrong meaning or confusion. Normally, no more than two or three verses should be combined.

    📖 John 4:7-8, 9 (REB) "His disciples had gone into the town to buy food. Meanwhile a Samaritan woman came to draw water, and Jesus said to her, 'Give me a drink.' The woman said, 'What! You, a Jew, ask for a drink from a Samaritan woman?'"

    📖 John 4:6b-8, 9 (CEV) "It was noon, and after Jesus' disciples had gone into town to buy some food, a Samaritan woman came to draw water from the well. Jesus asked her, 'Would you please give me a drink of water?' 'You are a Jew,' she replied, 'and I am a Samaritan woman. How can you ask me for a drink of water when Jews and Samaritans won't have anything to do with each other?'"

3. *Parenthesis.* A comment or event is added which is off the event line of the paragraph.

- 📖 John 21:7 (TEV) "When Peter heard that it was the Lord, he wrapped his outer garment around him (for he had taken his clothes off) and jumped into the water."
- 📖 Galatians 2:6 (NIV) "As for those who seemed to be important—whatever they were makes no difference to me; God does not judge by external appearance—those men added nothing to my message."

Problem: The parenthetical material leaves the reader confused as to how it relates to the rest of the narrative.

Solution: Rearrange the sentences so that the comment is no longer embedded in another clause and fits into the rest of the discourse.
- 📖 John 21:7 (CEV) "When Simon heard that it was the Lord, he put on the clothes that he had taken off while he was working. Then he jumped into the water."
- 📖 Galatians 2:6 (CEV) "Some of them were supposed to be important leaders, but I didn't care who they were. God doesn't have any favorites! None of these so-called special leaders added anything to my message."

CLARITY IN TRANSLATION

—the quality of a translation to plainly communicate the same message that the source text communicated to its original readers. The message needs to be in a form that can be easily understood by its readers.

Problem: The readers do not fully understand the translation. There may be obscure sentences, complicated grammar, or unintended ambiguities.

Solution: The translation must be revised until it is clearly and correctly understood by its readers. It is essential that a translation be thoroughly tested for reader comprehension before it is published. Some translation teams have a receptor language consultant whose work is to review the translation for smoothness, clarity, and readability.

COHESION/TRANSITION

—references to the proper relationship and connection between higher-level discourse units (i.e., units above the propositional level). This category includes deictic reference, but not participant reference, for which there is a specific category.

Problems:
1. The theme is not clear to the readers, or the discourse unit fails to flow smoothly as a whole and is perceived to be disjointed.

   Solution: The translator must utilize everything available in the language in order to produce the cohesion needed for effective communication. The cohesive devices of the language, such as conjunctions, pronouns, verb affixes, and special particles, must be understood and applied. The relational structure, lexical cohesion, pronoun use, genre type, and all the other features of a language must be utilized to produce a smooth, flowing discourse.

2. Transition words in the source language are kept in a translation when they are not appropriate in that language.
   📖 Mark 1:4-45 (KJV) Thirty-six of the verses begin with "and."

   Solution: Use the transition words, or lack of words, that are natural for the receptor language.
   📖 Mark 1:4-45 (CEV) None of the verses begin with "and." (Also ISV.)

COLLOCATION —the co-occurrence of words in a proper and meaningful way. In any language, each word has a limited range of words with which it may properly occur. It is not to be expected that a word in the source language will have the same collocational range as a word in the receptor language.

Problems:
1. The translator finds the proper equivalent for a word in one context, but in another context a collocational clash results when the same translation of the word is used.
   📖 Matthew 9:2 (NIV) "When Jesus *saw* their faith."
   📖 John 11:32 "When she saw him, she *fell* at his feet."
   📖 2 Thessalonians 3:1 "pray for us, that the word of the Lord may *run*."
   📖 2 John 6 (NIV) "his command is that you *walk* in love."

   Solution: Use the word that collocates correctly in each context.
   📖 Matthew 9:2 (TEV) "when Jesus *saw how much* faith they had." (Similarly CEV.)
   📖 John 11:32 (CEV) "As soon as she saw him, she *knelt at* his feet."

> 📖 2 Thessalonians 3:1 (NRSV) "pray for us, so that the word of the Lord may *spread rapidly*." (Similarly CEV, ISV, NCV, NET, NIV, NLT, NRSV, TEV.)
> (REB) "pray for us, that the word of the Lord may *have everywhere the swift and glorious success* it has had among you."
> 📖 2 John 6 (TEV) "The command ... is that you must all *live in love*." (Similarly NCV.)
> (NLT) "he has commanded us *to love* one another."
> (CEV) "he told you *to love* him."

2. Many figures of speech involve collocational clashes and are meaningful only if the reader recognizes that they are figures of speech.
   > 📖 Mark 1:5 (KJV) "And there *went out* unto him all the *land* of Judea."

Solution: See the various figures of speech under the topic RHETORIC.

COMPARATIVE RELATION

—the comparison of two items when one has more of something than the other. The grammatical devices used to signal comparative relation in the receptor language may be quite different from the devices found in the source language.

📖 Matthew 12:42 (NIV) "now one *greater than* Solomon is here."
📖 Luke 12:24 (NIV) "And how *much more valuable* you are *than* birds."
📖 Acts 27:11 (REB) "But the centurion paid *more attention* to the captain and to the owner of the ship *than* to what Paul said."
📖 Hebrews 7:7 (NIV) "the *lesser* person is blessed by the *greater*."

Problem: The receptor language does not make comparisons in the same way or use them for the same purposes as the source language.

Solutions: The way the language does make comparisons must be followed. Various solutions have been discovered.

   1. State that each item has the quality and use "very" to make the comparison.
      > 📖 Matthew 12:42 "Solomon was *great*. Now one who is *very great* is here."

   2. Make a negative statement about one of the items.
      > 📖 Luke 12:24 "Birds *are not very valuable*, but you *are valuable*."

📖 Acts 27:11 (NIV) "But the centurion, *instead of listening* to what Paul said, *followed* the advice of the pilot and of the owner of the ship."
(NCV) "But the captain and the owner of the ship *did not agree* with Paul, and the officer *believed* what the captain and owner of the ship said."
(ISV) "But the centurion *was persuaded by* the pilot and the owner of the ship *and not by* what Paul said."

3. Use an antonym for one of the items.
   📖 Hebrews 7:7 "The *unimportant* person is blessed by the *important* person."

CONDITION —an "if" clause, i.e., a clause that is dependent on a consequence. The condition may have a potential fact for a specific instance or a potential fact in a general or universal statement. The condition may state an obvious fact, or it may be a condition that never took place and never will take place.
📖 Matthew 12:27 (NRSV) "*If* I cast out demons by Beelzebul ..."
📖 John 20:15 (NRSV) "Sir, *if* you have carried him away, tell me where you have laid him."
📖 Mark 9:35 (NIV) "*If* anyone wants to be first, he must be the very last."
📖 1 Peter 3:14 (NIV) "But even *if* you should suffer for what is right, you are blessed."
📖 1 John 4:11 (TEV) "Dear friends, *if* this is how God loved us, then we should love one another."

Problem: The reader interprets all types of conditional sentences as being uncertain about their fulfillment.

Solutions: Translate each type of condition in the appropriate way for the receptor language. Often the different types of conditions will be expressed by different forms.

1. General conditions can be translated as general statements.
   📖 Mark 9:35 (TEV) "*Whoever* wants to be first must place himself last of all." (Similarly NCV, NRSV.)
   (NLT) "*Anyone who* wants to be the first must take last place and be the servant of everyone else."

2. Accomplished facts can be translated as reason or grounds clauses.

  📖 1 John 4:11 (NIV) "Dear friends, *since* God so loved us, we also ought to love one another." (Similarly CEV, NLT, NRSV.)

 3. Contrary-to-fact conditions can be translated so as to show that the speaker does not think the condition accords with the facts.
  📖 Matthew 12:27 (TEV) "*You say that* I drive out demons because Beelzebul gives me the power to do so. *Well, then*, who gives your followers the power to drive them out?" (Similarly NCV.)

CONNOTATION —the secondary meaning of a word or phrase triggering an emotional reaction. The hearer's reaction is often conditioned by the context in which the word is used, by the people associated with the word, or by his previous experiences.

Problem: A word that seems to be the proper equivalent to the concept in the source text is not accepted by the reader because he feels that it is improper to use it in that context.
  📖 John 19:26 (NRSV) "*Woman* [if such an address would indicate disrespect], here is your son."
  📖 Romans 1:1 (NET) "From Paul, a *slave* [when the primary connotation is harsh oppression] of Christ Jesus."
  📖 1 Corinthians 6:13 (KJV) "Meats for the *belly*, and the *belly* for meats."

Solution: Use the socially proper equivalent for the context in which the word is used.
  📖 John 19:26 (REB) "*Mother*, there is your son."
  (NIV) "*Dear woman*, here is your son." (Similarly NCV.)
  (CEV) "he said to his mother, 'This man is now your son.'" (Similarly TEV.)
  📖 Romans 1:1 (NRSV) "Paul, a *servant* of Jesus Christ." (Similarly CEV, ISV, KJV, NCV, NIV, NRSV, REB, TEV.)
  📖 1 Corinthians 6:13 (NIV) "Food for the *stomach* and the *stomach* for food." (Similarly ISV, NCV, NET, NLT, NRSV, TEV.)

CROSS-CULTURAL MISMATCH —the difference between the culture of the original writer and the culture of the people who read the translation.

Problem: The readers of the translation incorrectly interpret situations and references in terms of their own background. They may lack knowledge of the biblical background; they may interpret symbolic actions differently; they may have never known about objects mentioned in the Bible; their ideas of the spirit world may differ greatly from the spirit world referred to in the Bible.

Solution: Since new readers will understand the message in terms of their own backgrounds, express the message in a way that will be as meaningful as possible to them.

C**ROSS-REFERENCE** —a reference to another passage that has some connection with the text. The connection may be to a word, phrase, or a whole section. Note that references to parallel passages (i.e., passages in another Bible book that describe the same event or have essentially the same content) are in a separate category.

Problem: The translator wonders how many cross-references to include.

Solution: The amount of cross-references in major versions varies greatly and so a version with a great many cross-references does not justify putting a large number in the translation. Cross-references can be kept to a manageable number by using references to (1) the location of a passage that describes the historical event that is mentioned, (2) the location of the source of a quotation, (3) the location of the passage that is clearly alluded to, and (4) a parallel treatment of the same subject matter. This list works in both directions so that original accounts or quotations would have cross-references to where they are mentioned in other verses. The references are useful only when the reader can turn to the passages indicated, so they may be confined to books that have been translated and thus are available. If there are many bilingual readers, perhaps a limited number of references may also be made to books that are in the national language version.

D**ISCOURSE UNIT** —various levels of discourse units as defined by formal features. These help identify the boundaries of larger discourse units, such as sentences, paragraphs, sections, and other divisions.

Problems:
1. Readers seem to find it difficult to recognize the discourse units in the text.

Solution: The translator must use the proper receptor language paragraph markers and devices to indicate paragraph boundaries. The paragraph must use the proper features of cohesion, information load, tense sequence, participant reference, and relation markers.

2. The translation does not show the division of themes by presenting the text in semantic paragraphs. It might use the separate verse format of KJV, or it may break the text at places other than where the themes change.

Solution: Encourage the readers to read all the text concerned with one theme by formatting the paragraphs to correspond with the theme and its supporting sentences. Use the receptor language's paragraph system in presenting the material.

DOUBLE MEANING (author intended ambiguity) —the author's deliberate use of a word or phrase with a double meaning.

- John 3:3 "Truly, truly I say to you, unless someone is born *again/from above*, he is not able to see the kingdom of God."
- John 4:10–11 (NRSV) "'... and he would have given you *living* water.' The woman said to him ... 'Where do you get that *living* water?'"

Problem: The receptor language does not have a word with the same two senses that the word in the source language has.

Solution: Translate the one meaning that is most in focus and perhaps provide a footnote.
- John 3:3 (NRSV) "I tell you, no one can see the kingdom of God without being born from above." Footnote: "Or *born anew*." (Similarly CEV, ISV, NET.)
(NIV) "I tell you the truth, no one can see the kingdom of God unless he is born again." Footnote: "Or *born from above*." (Similarly NLT, TEV; without footnote NCV, REB.)
- John 4:10–11 (CEV) "'... you would ask him for the water that gives life.' 'Sir,' the woman said, 'you don't even have a bucket, and the well is deep. Where are you going to get this life-giving water?'"
(NET) Footnote: "The word translated *living* is used in Greek of flowing water, which leads to the woman's misunderstanding in the following verse. She thought Jesus was referring to some unknown source of drinkable water."

ELLIPSIS —a grammatical shortcut in which words or phrases are omitted from a discourse when the context makes it clear what the omitted words are. Some information is implied by the grammar of the passage. Information that already has been explicitly given can later be left implicit by an incomplete grammatical construction. Grammatical omissions allowed in the source language are not necessarily allowed in the receptor language. If ellipsis is used inappropriately in the translation, the reader of the translation might not get enough information from the text to understand it correctly.

- Matthew 26:4–5 (NIV) "and they plotted to arrest Jesus in some sly way and kill him. '*But not* during the Feast,' they said, 'or there may be a riot among the people.'"
- John 15:4 (NRSV) "Just as the branch cannot bear fruit by itself unless it abides in the vine, neither *can you* unless you abide in me."
- Romans 14:2 (NRSV) "Some believe in eating anything, while the *weak* eat only vegetables."

Problem: Grammatical omissions allowed in one language are not necessarily allowed in another language. The reader of the translation might not get enough information from the text to understand it correctly.

Solution: Supply words that are implied from the context.
- Matthew 26:4–5 (NCV) "At the meeting they planned to set a trap to arrest Jesus and kill him. But they said, '*We must not do it* during the feast, because the people might cause a riot.'" (Similarly CEV, ISV, REB.)
- John 15:4 (NIV) "No branch can bear fruit by itself; it must remain in the vine. Neither *can you bear fruit* unless you remain in me." (Similarly NCV, NLT, REB, TEV.)
- Romans 14:2 (TEV) "One person's faith allows him to eat anything, but the person who is *weak in the faith* [from 14:1] eats only vegetables." (Similarly CEV, NIV.)
 (NLT) "For instance, one person believes it is all right to eat anything. But another believer who *has a sensitive conscience* will eat only vegetables."

EMOTIVE FOCUS —the effect or impact that the translation has on the emotions of the reader or hearer. If the original message was dramatic and exciting, the translation should also be dramatic and exciting. If the original message made people feel sad, the translation should also make people feel sad.

Problem: As the translator tries to express the meaning of a passage accurately and clearly, the emotional force of the original is lost or skewed.

Solution: Translate in a way that retains the emotional impact of the original. Consider how the people involved in the original situation must have felt and find out how to express those feelings in the translation. Use what is natural to achieve this emotional impact for the receptor language, e.g., with idioms, figures of speech, exclamations, etc.

EUPHEMISM

—the use of an agreeable and inoffensive word or expression in place of one that is indelicate, offensive, holy, or taboo. Included is the Jewish custom of showing reverence for God by avoiding the use of the word "God" and substituting "heaven" or some attribute of God.

📖 1 Corinthians 7:1 (NRSV) "It is well for a man not to *touch* a woman."

📖 Matthew 21:25 (NIV) "John's baptism—where did it come from? Was it from *heaven*, or from men?"

📖 Matthew 26:64 (TEV) "you will see the Son of Man sitting at the right side of the *Almighty*."

Problems: (1) The reader of the translation does not recognize that the expression is figurative and takes the statement literally. (2) The reader recognizes that the statement is not to be taken literally, but does not properly relate the figurative expression with its intended meaning.

Solutions:
1. Use a euphemism that is natural to the receptor language.
    📖 1 Corinthians 7:1 (TEV) "A man does well not to *marry*." (Similarly CEV, NIV.)
    (NLT) "Yes, it is good *to live a celibate life*."

2. Use a nonfigurative expression.
    📖 1 Corinthians 7:1 (REB) "It is a good thing for a man not to *have intercourse* with a woman."
    (NCV) "It is good for a man not *to have sexual relations* with a woman."
    📖 Matthew 21:25 (TEV) "Where did John's right to baptize come from: was it from *God* or from man?" (Similarly NCV, REB.)
    (CEV) "Who gave John the right to baptize? Was it *God in heaven* or merely some human being?"

📖 Matthew 26:64 (CEV) "Soon you will see the Son of Man sitting at the right side of *God* All-Powerful."
(NLT) "And in the future you will see me, the Son of Man, sitting at *God's* right hand in the place of power."

FIGURATIVE EXTENSION —a word or expression that stands for another because of their close association.

a. *Metonymy*. The use of one expression for another because the two referents are associated in some way or because one suggests the other.
   📖 Mark 3:25 (NIV) "If a *house* is divided against itself" [the place for those who live in it].
   📖 Mark 9:17 (KJV) "which hath a *dumb* spirit" [the effect as though an attribute of the agent].
   📖 Acts 8:28 (NRSV) "he was reading the *prophet* Isaiah" [the writer for his writing].
   📖 1 Corinthians. 3:13 (NRSV) "for the *Day* will disclose it" [the time for what will take place at that time].

   Problems: (1) The reader of the translation does not recognize that the expression is figurative and takes the statement literally. (2) The reader recognizes that the statement is not to be taken literally, but does not properly relate the figurative expression with its intended meaning.

   Solution: Make the implied association explicit.
   📖 Mark 3:25 (TEV) "If a *family* divides itself into groups which fight each other." (Similarly CEV, NCV.)
   (ISV) "And if a *household* is divided against itself." (Similarly REB.)
   📖 Mark 9:17 (NRSV) "he has a spirit *that makes him unable to speak*." (Similarly CEV, ISV, NCV, NET, NIV, NLT, REB, TEV.)
   📖 Acts 8:28 (TEV) "he was reading from *the book of the prophet* Isaiah." (Similarly CEV, NCV, NIV, NLT.)
   📖 1 Corinthians 3:13 (TEV) "For on that Day *fire* will reveal everyone's work." (Similarly CEV.)

b. *Synecdoche*. A part of something is used to refer to the whole thing, or (less commonly) the whole is used to refer to a part of that thing.
   📖 Matthew 6:11 (NIV) "Give us today our daily *bread*."
   📖 John 1:19 (NIV) "the *Jews* of Jerusalem sent priests and Levites to ask him who he was."

Problems: (1) The reader of the translation does not recognize that the expression is figurative and takes the statement literally. (2) The reader recognizes that the statement is not to be taken literally, but does not properly relate the figurative expression with its intended meaning.

Solutions: Enlarge the part to the intended whole, or reduce the whole to the part that was intended.
- Matthew 6:11 (TEV) "Give us today the *food* we need." (Similarly CEV, NCV, NLT.)
- John 1:19 (TEV) "The *Jewish authorities* in Jerusalem sent some priests and Levites to John to ask him, 'Who are you?'" (Similarly CEV, NET, NLT.)

FOOTNOTE —a note at the bottom of the page that gives information needed for a better understanding of the text or information on alternative interpretations and variant manuscript readings. Footnotes need to be brief and easy to distinguish from the main part of the text. If a long note is required, it should usually be treated as a glossary item at the back of the book.

Problems: Items in the text of the translation need explanations to be understandable.

Solution: Use footnotes to supply essential information for understanding (1) the meaning or sound of a person's name, (2) geographic locations, (3) historical background, (4) information contained in another part of the Bible, (5) unfamiliar customs, (6) unknown objects or occupations, (7) puzzling statements, (8) explanations of a figure of speech or symbolic use of a word, (9) literal translations, (10) alternative interpretations, and (11) textual variants.
- (1) Matthew 27:46-47 (ISV) "About three o'clock Jesus cried out in a loud voice, 'Eli, Eli, lema sabachthani?', which means, 'My God, my God, why have you forsaken me?' When some of the people standing there heard this, they said, 'He's calling for Elijah.'" Footnote: "Elijah in Heb. sounds like *Eli*." (Similarly CEV.)
- (2) Luke 5:1 (CEV) "Jesus was standing on the shore of Lake Gennesaret." Footnote: "Another name for Lake Galilee." (Similarly NET, NIV.)
- (3) Acts 12:1 (CEV) "At that time King Herod caused terrible suffering for some members of the church." Footnote: "Herod

Agrippa I, the grandson of Herod the Great." (Similarly NET, NLT, TEV.)

📖 (4) Luke 17:32 (CEV) "Remember what happened to Lot's wife." Footnote: "She turned to a block of salt when she disobeyed God." (Similarly NCV.)

📖 (5) Luke 22:47 (CEV) "He went over to Jesus and greeted him with a kiss." Footnote: "It was the custom for people to greet each other with a kiss on the cheek."

📖 (6) Matthew 23:5 (ISV) "They increase the size of their phylacteries." Footnote: "I.e. leather cases containing Scripture texts." (Similarly CEV, NCV, NET, NIV.)

📖 (7) Romans 16:22 (CEV) "I, Tertius, also send my greetings. I am a follower of the Lord, and I wrote this letter." Footnote: "Paul probably dictated this letter to Tertius."

📖 (8) James 1:1 (CEV) "Greetings to the twelve tribes scattered all over the world." Footnote: "James is saying that the Lord's followers are like the tribe of Israel that were scattered everywhere by their enemies." (Similarly NET.)

📖 (9) Matthew 20:20 (CEV) "The mother of James and John came to Jesus with her two sons." Footnote: "The Greek text has 'mother of the sons of Zebedee' (see 26.37)."

📖 (10) John 3:3 (NLT) "Jesus replied, 'I assure you, unless you are born again, you can never see the kingdom of God.'" Footnote: "Or *born from above*, also in 3:7." (Similarly NIV, TEV.) (CEV) "Jesus replied, 'I tell you for certain that you must be born from above before you can see God's kingdom.'" Footnote: "Or 'in a new way.' The same Greek word is used in verses 7, 31." Similarly ISV, NET, NRSV.)

📖 (11) 1 Corinthians 11:24 (ISV) "This is my body that is for you." Footnote: "Other mss. read *that is broken*; still other mss. read *that is given*." (Similarly NLT, NRSV.)

FORM —a form in the source text that has meaning in itself, for example, acrostics and paronomasia.

Problems:
1. The clever use of the spelling of words in acrostic poetry where the first letter of every line or verse combine to form the alphabet (Psalms 9–10, 25, 34, 111, 112, and 119) and word play in the original languages cannot be duplicated in the receptor language.

Solution: Words and their spellings are language specific and the forms of the words do not carry through in translation. Translating the meaning is sufficient in this case.

2. Paronomasia is a play on words by using two similar and closely related words that are similar in pronunciation. Since this involves the form of the word, it cannot usually be duplicated in the receptor language.

Solution: This word play cannot be duplicated in translation, but if it is significant to the meaning of the passage, a footnote can explain it.

📖 Genesis 2:7 (TEV) "Then the LORD God took some soil from the ground and formed a man out of it." Footnote: "The Hebrew words for 'man' and 'ground' have similar sounds."

(REB) "The LORD God formed a human being from the dust of the ground." Footnote: "human being: *Heb*. adam. ground: *Heb*. adamah."

FORMULA —set forms used to mark certain discourse forms. This includes prophetic announcement ("thus says the Lord") and Paul's epistle openings.

📖 Jeremiah 30:5 (KJV) "For thus saith the LORD: . . ."

📖 Colossians 1:1-2 (NIV) "Paul, an apostle of Christ Jesus by the will of God, and Timothy our brother, to the holy and faithful brothers in Christ at Colosse."

Problem: A formula for a certain type of discourse is translated in different ways so that it is not apparent that a certain form for introducing the discourse was employed in the original.

Solution: Once the formula is modified to communicate the meaning naturally, keep the same pattern throughout so that it can be recognized as an introduction to a particular type of discourse.

📖 Jeremiah 30:5 (NIV) "This is what the LORD says: . . ."

📖 Colossians 1:1-2 (NLT) "This letter is from Paul, chosen by God to be an apostle of Christ Jesus and from our brother Timothy. It is written to God's holy people in the city of Colosse."

FRONT AND BACK MATTER —supplementary information at the front or back of the book. This includes maps, tables, and contents. Such material is often helpful for understanding the books of the Bible.

Problem: The book titles are not planned to make it clear how they are related to each other.

Solution: The traditional ordering of the NT books has a built-in grouping that can be made explicit for the reader in the contents page. There are four main divisions of the books which can have long titles. The individual books may have to be shortened to fit the page. For example:

This is about the Good News concerning Jesus Christ
    This is what Matthew wrote
    This is what Mark wrote
    Etc.
This is how the apostles of Jesus Christ spread the Good News
These are letters written to those who believed in Jesus Christ
    The letters written by Paul
        The letter written to the believers in Rome
        Etc:
    The letter written to the believers who are Hebrews
    The letter written by James
    Etc.
This is what Jesus Christ revealed to John about what was to happen

GENITIVE IN SOURCE TEXT

—two words or phrases occurring together in Hebrew or Greek (or in an intermediate source language), one of which is in the genitive case to indicate that it is related in some way to the other. This construction is often symbolized *A of B*, with "of B" indicating that B is in the genitive case. Genitive constructions in the source text may signal various meanings other than ownership (e.g., identification, kinship, location, or content) It is important that the translation communicate the meaning intended in the source text.

Problem: The receptor language does not have an equivalent genitive construction, or it may have a similar construction that does not cover the same range of relationships as found in Greek and fails to communicate the correct meaning.

Solution: State the relationships between A and B clearly. For the construction *A of B,* determine the semantic word classes for both *A* and *B* (See SKEWING BETWEEN GRAMMAR AND SEMANTICS). If there is an attribute, determine what it modifies. Then determine the identity of the participants in the events. Finally, put together all the elements involved, including implied events or states, in the way the receptor language best communicates the meaning.

- Matthew 12:31 "the blasphemy of the Spirit" [event + thing = (whoever) blasphemes the Spirit].
  (NLT) "blasphemy *against* the Holy Spirit." (Similarly ISV, NET, NIV, NRSV, REB.)
  (NCV) "whoever speaks *against* the Holy Spirit." (Similarly CEV.)
  (TEV) "whoever says evil things *against* the Holy Spirit."
- Mark 1:4 "a baptism of repentance" [event + event = (people) should repent (and show this by) being baptized (by John)].
  (NLT) "people should be baptized *to show that* they had turned from their sins and turned to God."
  (TEV) "Turn away from your sins *and* be baptized." (Similarly CEV.)
  (REB) "a baptism *in token of* repentance."
- Luke 1:17 "the power of Elijah" [attribute + thing = the power (possessed by or shown by) Elijah].
  (CEV) "He will go ahead of the Lord *with the same* power and spirit *that Elijah had.*" (Similarly NCV, TEV.)
- John 6:35 "the bread of life" [thing + event = the bread (that causes people) to live].
  (NCV) "I am the bread *that gives life.*" (Similarly CEV.)
- Acts 2:38 "the gift of the Holy Spirit" [thing-event + thing = (Christ) will give (you) the Holy Spirit].
  (CEV) "then you *will be given* the Holy Spirit."
  (TEV) "you *will receive* God's gift, the Holy Spirit." (Similarly ISV.)
- Romans 15:26 "the poor of the saints" [thing-attribute + thing-attribute = the poor people (among) the holy people].
  (NCV) "the poor *among* God's people." (Similarly ISV, NET, NIV, NRSV, REB, TEV.)
- Ephesians 2:8 "the gift of God" [thing-event + thing = what God gives (you)].
  (NLT) "a gift *from God*" (Similarly NCV.)
  (CEV) "*God's* gift to you." (Similarly REB, TEV.)

GENRE —the type of literary composition. Different types of speech are appropriate in different situations. If the writer is exhorting his readers, certain linguistic forms are appropriate; if he is arguing or passing on information, other forms need to be used. The main genre types are (1) narrative discourse, which recounts events; (2) procedural discourse, which tells how to do something; (3) expository discourse, which explains or argues; (4) descriptive discourse, which describes some topic; (5) hortatory discourse, which suggests or commands actions; and (6) repartee or conversational discourse, which recounts speech exchanges. A long text will probably have a mixture of genres. A Gospel is basically a narrative discourse which includes repartee. In its speech quotations, there are expository and hortatory discourses. Galatians is an expository discourse which includes a section of narrative discourse.

Problem: A translation does not take into account the appropriate types of discourse features for the receptor language and so the translation is unnatural or unclear. For example, a language might require the full setting be given first before describing the sequence of events in a narrative, yet Greek often introduces parts of the setting after the narrative has begun.

Solution: Determine how the particular genre is presented in the receptor language. For the different types, study person orientation in presenting the material, the involvement of the writer and the person addressed, normal sentence length, paragraph structure, and the normal tense used. The type of discourse in the source language should be presented as the receptor language would present it. If it is appropriate for the full setting to be given at the beginning of a narrative, then information given further on in the text of the source language can be moved to the beginning.

GLOSSARY

—a section at the back of the book that explains unknown ideas used in the translation. The list can include people (Aaron, Isaac, Moses), festivals (Pentecost, Passover), professions (prophet, scribe, lawyer), titles (Messiah, Son of Man, Son of David), customs (circumcision, fasting, washing hands), and other unknown things (myrrh, phylactery, wreath).

Problems:
1. The translator does not know how to indicate that a word in the text is explained in the glossary.

    Solution: An asterisk is often used to mark a word that is explained in the glossary. However, the words in the text do not have to be marked. If the glossary is well constructed so that it is easy to read from item to item, readers may use it for supplementary study and either learn the contents or realize that they can probably find help there when puzzled about a word.

2. The translator does not know what items to include in a glossary.

Solution: Right from the start, a translator needs to be making a list of the items that will require supplemental information. The list will be different for each language. Items commonly included in glossaries that are translated in a meaningful way often will not need to appear. Words that require more information than provided by the translation are candidates for a glossary. Supplementary information is not confined to glossaries since book introductions, footnotes, section headings, picture captions, and maps also provided information. Even the single book that is first printed should include a glossary that is relevant to that book. This will help test the glossary and also train readers to use it.

Hendiadys
—two nouns connected by "and" when, semantically, one is in a subordinate, instead of coordinate, relationship with the other.
- Acts 1:25 (NRSV) "to take the place in this *ministry and apostleship.*"
- Acts 23:6 (KJV) "of *the hope and resurrection of the dead* I am called in question."
- 2 Timothy 1:10 (NRSV) "who abolished death and brought *life and immortality* to light through the gospel."

Problem: The receptor language does not join two concepts with "and" when they are not coordinate.

Solutions:
1. Translate an attribute as an adjective or phrase modifying the noun.
   - Acts 1:25 (NIV) "to take over this *apostolic ministry.*"
   - 2 Timothy 1:10 (TEV) "He has ended the power of death and through the gospel has revealed *immortal life.*" (Similarly NLT.)
   (NCV) "He destroyed death, and through the good News he showed us the way to have *life that cannot be destroyed.*"
   (CEV) ". . . and offers *life that never ends.*"

2. Translate an event noun as a verb.
   - Acts 1:25 (TEV) *"to serve as an apostle."*
   - Acts 23:6 (CEV) "I am on trial simply because *I believe that the dead will be raised to life.*"
   (NIV) "I stand on trial *because of my hope in the resurrection of the dead.*" (Similarly CEV, NCV, NLT, TEV.)

HYPERBOLE

HYPERBOLE —a statement that exaggerates for the sake of emphasis.

- Matthew 11:18 (NIV) "For John came *neither eating nor drinking.*"
- Mark 1:5 (NIV) "The *whole* Judean countryside and *all* the people of Jerusalem went out to him."
- Luke 14:26 (NIV) "If anyone comes to me and does not *hate* his father and mother . . . he cannot be my disciple."

Problems: (1) The reader of the translation does not recognize that the expression is figurative and takes the statement literally. (2) The reader recognizes that the statement is not to be taken literally, but does not properly relate the figurative expression with its intended meaning.

Solution: State what is actually meant.
- Matthew 11:18 (TEV) "When John came, he *fasted* and *drank no wine.*"
  (NLT) "John the Baptist *didn't drink wine* and he *often fasted.*"
- Mark 1:5 (TEV) "*Many* people from the province of Judea and the city of Jerusalem went out to hear John."
  (CEV) "From all Judea and Jerusalem *crowds* of people went to John."
- Luke 14:26 (NCV) "If anyone comes to me but *loves* his father, mother . . . *more than* me, he cannot be my follower."
  (CEV) "You cannot be my disciple unless you love me *more than* you love your father and mother . . ." (Similarly NLT.)

IDIOM —a fixed combination of words, the meaning of which is derived from perceiving the unit as a whole rather than as individual words. These are often dead metaphors: a comparison is no longer intended.
- John 11:41 (KJV) "Jesus *lifted up his eyes.*"
- Acts 2:37 (NIV) "they *were cut to the heart.*"

Problem: The translator translates the individual words or attempts to treat the idiom as a metaphor or some other figure of speech.

Solution: Translate the equivalent meaning of the unit. Conversely, idioms in the receptor language should be used when they are the proper equivalents for words or phrases in the source language.
- John 11:41 (NIV) "Jesus *looked up.*" (Also ISV, NCV, NET, NRSV, REB, TEV.)
  (NLT) "Jesus *looked up to heaven.*"
- Acts 2:37 (TEV) "they *were deeply troubled.*"

(NET) "they *were acutely distressed.*"
(CEV) "they *were very upset.*"
(NCV) "they *felt guilty.*"
(NLT) "Peter's words *convicted them deeply.*"

ILLOCUTIONARY FORCE —the purpose for a clause or sentence, that is, its function in making a statement, asking a question, making a request, giving an order, making a promise, etc. Normally, the illocutionary force is the same as the grammatical mood of the sentence: a statement occurs as a declarative sentence, a question occurs as an interrogative sentence, and a command occurs as an imperative sentence. Languages may skew these correspondences so that declarative sentences will sometimes communicate commands or questions, interrogative sentences may communicate statements or commands, and imperative sentences may communicate statements or questions.

Problems:
1. The reader does not understand that a declarative sentence should be taken as a command instead of a mere prediction.
    - Matthew 1:21 (TEV) "She will have a son, and you *will* name him Jesus."
    - 3 John 6 (NIV) "You will *do well* to send them on their way in a manner worthy of God."

    Solution: Translate the intended command as a command or a polite request.
    - Matthew 1:21 (NIV) "She will give birth to a son, and you *are to* give him the name Jesus." (Similarly CEV, ISV, NLT, NRSV.)
    - 3 John 6 (TEV) "*Please help* them to continue their trip in a way that will please God." (Similarly NCV, REB.)

2. The reader does not understand that an imperative sentence should be taken as a condition instead of a command.
    - John 2:19 (NIV) "*Destroy* this temple, and I will raise it again in three days."

    Solution: If the irony cannot be captured, translate as a condition.
    - John 2:19 "*If you destroy* this temple, I will raise it again in three days."

IMPLICATURE —information that is not overtly stated in words in the source text, but which nevertheless is communicated as part of the total message. This may include implicatures communicated through figures of speech, or through the description of a sequence of events. While some languages may make each step of an argument explicit, others may jump some logical steps but the hearer must know that they are implied. An implicature is the information conveyed by the act of implication.

📖 Matthew 2:2 (NRSV) "Where is the child who has been born king of the Jews? *For* we observed his star at its rising."

📖 Matthew 4:6 (TEV) "If you are God's Son, throw yourself down, *for* the scripture says, ... 'not even your feet will be hurt on the stones.'"

📖 Matthew 6:26 (NIV) "Look at the birds of the air; they do not sow or reap or store away in barns, and yet your heavenly Father feeds them. Are you not much more valuable than they?"

Problems:

1. The reader of the translation does not get enough information from the text to understand the argument correctly.

    Solution: Supply the implied steps from the context.

    📖 Matthew 2:2 "Where is the child who has been born king of the Jews? *We know that a king has been born* for we have seen his star at its rising."

    📖 Matthew 4:6 "If you are God's son, throw yourself down. *You can do so and not be hurt,* for the scripture says, '... not even your feet will be hurt on the stones.'"

    📖 Matthew 6:26 "... Are you not much more valuable than they? *Therefore your heavenly Father will surely provide for you too.*"

2. Material is added in the translation which, although true in the context of the entire Bible, is not linguistically implicit in the near context of the passage.

    📖 1 John 2:4 (LB) "Someone may say, '*I am a Christian; I am on my way to heaven;* I belong to Christ.'"

    Solution: Omit the extraneous material.

3. Cultural background material is included in the translation which could be considered part of the knowledge shared by the writer and the original readers, but is not pertinent to the focus of the passage.

    📖 Acts 20:6 "But we sailed away from Philippi after the Feast of Unleavened Bread *when the Jews celebrate their ancient deliverance from Egypt.*"

Solution: Omit the extraneous material.

4. Explicit information in the source text is considered to be redundant by readers in the receptor language.
   📖 Matthew 8:20 (NIV) "Foxes have holes and birds *of the air* have nests."

   Solution: Omit the redundant material.
   📖 Matthew 8:20 (CEV) "Foxes have dens, and birds have nests." (Similarly ISV, NCV, NLT, REB, TEV.)

INFLUENCE —factors that seem to be affecting the translation, such as theological bias, translation philosophy, third-language interference, and sociolinguistic setting of the translation project.

Problems:

1. The translator chooses an interpretation that is in conflict with an interpretation considered to be important by a denomination and it is likely that the translation will not be used because of this.
   📖 2 Cor. 5:14 "We are convinced that one has died *in the place of* [Presbyterian or Calvinistic interpretation] all, therefore all have died." versus "We are convinced that one has died *for the benefit of* [Methodist or Arminian interpretation] all, therefore all have died."

   Solution: Use ambiguous terms that can be accepted by all or put the preferred interpretation in the text of the translation, giving the alternative interpretation in a footnote.
   📖 2 Cor. 5:14 (NIV) "we are convinced that one died *for* all, and therefore all died."

2. The translator chooses a textual variant that is different from that used in the national language version and there are groups of readers who will compare the translations and criticize the new one for being different from the established version.

   Solution: Follow the text with the best justification and try to help the church leaders to understand the reason for that choice. The alternative text can be put in a footnote.
   📖 1 John 5:7-8 (NLT) "So we have these three witnesses*—the Spirit, the water, and the blood—and all three agree." Footnote: "Some very late manuscripts add *in heaven—the Father, the Word, and the Holy Spirit, and these three are one. And we have three witnesses on earth.*" (Similarly ISV, NET, NIV, NRSV.)

3. One of the translators wants to include a great deal of implicit information and background information in the text of the translation while others involved in the translation think that it should be closer to the text of the national translation.

   Solution: Instruct the people involved in the translation and the sponsors of the translation on the principles of meaning-based translation. Show them how footnotes can provide needed information that wasn't strictly communicated in the text of the original.

4. The translation team and their sponsors are not agreed about translation philosophy, some tending toward a literal approach and some toward a meaning-based approach.

   Solution: Provide orientation to the process of translation and provide convincing proof about the adequacy of a translation by testing it for correct communication with ordinary readers.

INFORMATION LOAD —the rate at which new information is presented in a text. Different languages communicate information at different rates and a translation should present information at the rate readers are accustomed to receiving it. Whether information is new to the hearers or already known by them is also a factor.

Problem: The reader is overwhelmed with references to new ideas, unknown objects, unfamiliar events, and strange customs. The point of the passage is lost in the mass of details.

Solution: The new objects and events need to be introduced in the text in a way that will not distract the reader from the main theme of the passage. Unknown information needs to presented at a slower rate. Some background material can be supplied outside the text in introductions, glossaries, and footnotes. More redundancy slows down the rate, but only natural patterns of redundancy should be used.

INTERPRETATION OF SOURCE TEXT —the meaning of the source text. The meaning may not be obvious, or there may be more than one possible interpretation and the translator has to choose which is the meaning that the author intended.

Problems:
1. The translator misunderstands the meaning of the passage.

📖 John 7:17 (KJV) "If any man *will do his will*, he shall know of the doctrine, whether it be of God, or whether I speak of myself," may have been translated to mean "If anyone *will do what God wants*, then he shall know ..."

Solution: Follow the interpretation that has the best justification. It is unlikely that a translator will have a valid interpretation if it has not previously been supported by biblical scholars. A translator needs to present very convincing reasons for a unique interpretation.

📖 John 7:17 (TEV) "whoever is *willing to do what God wants* will know whether what I teach comes from God or whether I speak on my own authority." (Similarly CEV, ISV, NET, NLT.)

(REB) "Whoever *chooses to do the will* of God will know whether my teaching comes from him or is merely my own." (Similarly NIV.)

2. The translator does not know which of several interpretations was intended by the original writer. All seem to fit the context equally well.

📖 John 14:1 (CEV) "Don't be worried! Have faith in God and have faith in me" (with two imperatives "have faith"). (Similarly CEV, ISV, NCV, NIV, NRSV, TEV.)

(KJV) "Let not your heart be troubled: ye believe in God, believe also in me," (with an indicative "ye believe" and an imperative "believe"). (Similarly NET, NLT.)

Solution: In a few instances translators might be able to translate with the same ambiguity they find in the original, but in most instances the language will not provide readers with the same choices of interpretation that the Greek allows. However, even if it were possible to translate ambiguously, the translation should not make it appear that the original writer was deliberately trying to be obscure or ambiguous. We assume that one meaning was intended to be communicated to the original recipients. Modern-day scholars must cope with hundreds of ambiguities because they are not participants of the historical setting and are not native speakers of the language as it was spoken at that period. Therefore, one interpretation should be chosen and alternatives can be put in footnotes if necessary. It is better to follow one interpretation clearly in the text than to translate in such a way that obscures meaning.

📖 John 14:1 (NRSV) "Do not let your hearts be troubled. Believe in God, believe also in me." Footnote: "Or *You believe*." (Similarly CEV, ISV, NIV, TEV.)

IRONY —a statement that expresses the speaker's attitude as being the opposite of the literal sense of the words.

1. It may be used to point out the foolishness of the one addressed, in order to teach or rebuke him.
   📖 1 Corinthians 4:8 (NRSV) "Already you have all you want!"
   📖 2 Corinthians 11:5 (CEV) "I think I am as good as any of those *super apostles*."

2. It may be sarcasm with the elements of bitterness or the desire to hurt.
   📖 John 19:14 (NIV) "Here is *your* King."

3. It may be jeering with the desire to make one appear foolish by taunting him.
   📖 Mark 15:32 (NRSV) "Let the Messiah, the King of Israel, come down from the cross now, so that we may see and believe."

Problems: (1) The reader of the translation does not recognize that the expression is figurative and takes the statement literally. (2) The reader recognizes that the statement is not to be taken literally, but does not properly relate the figurative expression with its intended meaning.

Solution: Give clues that irony is intended by adding attitudes, or enclosing it in quotation marks..
   📖 1 Corinthians 4:8 (NLT) "You *think* you already have everything you need!" (Similarly NCV.)
   📖 2 Corinthians 11:5 (NLT) "But I don't think I am inferior to these '*super apostles*.'" (Similarly ISV, NCV, NET, NIV.)
   (TEV) "I do not think that I am the least bit inferior to those *very special so-called 'apostles'* of yours!"
   📖 John 19:14 "Here is *your kind of* king."
   📖 Mark 15:32 "Let him *who says* he is the Messiah, the King of Israel, come down from the cross now if he wants us to believe in him."
   (NCV) "If he is *really* the Christ, the king of Israel, let him come down now from the cross. When we see this, we will believe in him."

KEY BIBLICAL TERM —an important word or expression in the Jewish or Christian beliefs and religious systems, or one that is used in a special way in the Bible. The proper translation of such terms is very important for communicating the biblical message without distorting it.

Problem: A term has been translated before the translator has studied it enough to provide the best equivalent.

Solution: The meaning of each key term needs to be thoroughly studied. The term should be compared with other biblical terms that have similar meanings to determine the important distinctions between them. The most appropriate equivalent is then chosen and tested to see how readers will understand it. *Key Biblical Terms in the New Testament* by Barnwell, Dancy, and Pope lists key terms, discusses their meanings, and suggests ways to translate them. Also see the suggestions given under UNKNOWN IDEA.

LAYOUT IN RL —the appearance of the publication in the receptor language. This includes the number of columns on a page, the font size of the various elements, the addition of a bilingual text, and the placement of page numbers and verse references.

Problem: The translator had not planned for this by the time the book is ready to be submitted for publication.

Solution: Samples of various acceptable styles need to be available. A consultant for printing books should be available to recommend a style and to warn of problems that the translator is not aware of.

LEXICAL CORRESPONDENCE —the range of meaning of a word in one language as compared with the range of meaning of its "equivalent" word in another language. Different senses of a source language word may sometimes need to be translated by different expressions in the receptor language. However, the same word in the source language should be translated consistently by the same word in the receptor language, except where there is a reason for not doing so.

Problems:
1. Key terms and parallel passages are translated in different ways when the contexts call for the same meaning.

   Solution: Check the items with a concordance to see that the best terms are used consistently. The FIESTA computer program has a check list for many key biblical terms. A harmony of the

Gospels will help in checking parallel passages. Especially helpful are the *Synopsis of the Four Gospels* edited by Kurt Aland (New York: United Bible Societies, 1982) and *The Horizontal Line Synopsis of the Gospels* by Reuben J. Swanson (Pasadena: William Carey Library, 1984).

2. Each occurrence of a word in the source language is translated by one word in the translation without regard to changes in the area of meaning.
   - Mark 12:15 (KJV) "Why *tempt* ye me?"; Acts 15:10 (KJV) "Now therefore why *tempt* ye God?"; James 1:13 (KJV) "God cannot *be tempted* with evil, neither *tempteth* he any man."
   - Luke 24:39 (KJV) "a spirit hath not *flesh* and bones"; John 1:14 (KJV) "the Word was made *flesh*"' Acts 2:17 (KJV) "I will pour out my Spirit upon all *flesh*"; Romans 8:3 (KJV) "it was weak through the *flesh*"; 2 Corinthians 10:3 (KJV) "though we walk in the *flesh*, we do not war after the *flesh*"; 1 Corinthians 1:26 (KJV) "not many wise men after the *flesh*."

   Solution: The word must be considered in context in order to determine the correct equivalent.
   - Mark 12:15 (TEV) "Why are you trying to *trap* me?"; Acts 15:10 (TEV) "So then, why do you now want *to put* God *to the test?*"; James 1:13 (TEV) "For God cannot *be tempted* by evil, and he himself *tempts* no one."
   - Luke 24:39 (CEV) "Ghosts don't have *flesh* and bones"; John 1:14 (CEV) "The Word became *a human being*"; Acts 2:17 (CEV) "I will give my Spirit to *everyone*"; Romans 8:3 (CEV) "*our selfish desires* make the Law weak"; 2 Corinthians 10:3 (CEV) "We live in *this world*, but we don't act like *its people*"; 1 Corinthians 1:26 (CEV) "*The people of this world* didn't think that many of you were wise."

3. The seemingly equivalent word used in the translation carries incomplete information if a crucial component is missing.
   - John 3:18 (TEV) "whoever does not believe has already been *judged*."

   Solution: Use a closer equivalent.
   - John 3:18 (NIV) "whoever does not believe *stands condemned* [since the judgment is adverse] already." (Similarly CEV, ISV, NET, NRSV.)
   (NCV) "Those who do not believe have already been *judged guilty*."

4. The seemingly equivalent word carries extraneous information if components are communicated that were not intended.
   📖 Mark 10:17 (NRSV) "Good Teacher, what must I do to *inherit* eternal life?"

   Solution: Use a closer equivalent.
   📖 Mark 10:17 (TEV) "Good Teacher, what must I do to *receive* [since there is no death or transfer of property involved] eternal life?"; (NLT) "to *get*"; (CEV) "to *have*"; (REB) "to *win*."

5. No equivalent word can be found in the receptor language for a concept already known by the speakers of the language.

   Solutions:
   1. Consider using a different word class.
      📖 Mark 1:4 (NIV) "a *baptism* of *repentance* for the *forgiveness* of sins" could have the event nouns translated as verbs: (TEV) "*Turn away from your sins* and *be baptized*... and God *will forgive* your sins." (Similarly CEV.)
      (NLT) "and was preaching that people should *be baptized* to show that they *had turned from their sins and turned to God* to *be forgiven*."

   2. Consider using a phrase or idiom already in use.
      📖 Acts 17:21 (NIV) "All the Athenians and the foreigners who lived there spent their time doing nothing but talking about and listening to the latest ideas." Here the one Greek word *eukairoun* is translated with the phrase "they spend their time."
      📖 Romans 13:9 (NRSV) "You shall not *commit adultery*" translates the one Greek word *moicheuseis* with the phrase "commit adultery."

   3. Consider using the negation of its antonym.
      📖 James 4:6 (NRSV) "but gives grace to the *humble*" could be translated "but gives grace to *those who are not proud*."

   4. Consider using a reciprocal verb.
      📖 Matthew 11:29 (NRSV) "Take my yoke upon you, and *learn* from me" could be translated "Take my yoke upon you, and let me *teach* you."

LITOTES

LITOTES —an emphatic affirmation of a fact by denying its opposite.
- Luke 1:37 (CEV) *"Nothing is impossible* for God."
- Acts 15:2 (NRSV) "Paul and Barnabas *had no small dissension and debate* with them."
- Acts 20:12 (NRSV) "Meanwhile they had taken the boy away alive and *were not a little* comforted."

Problems: The reader of the translation is puzzled about the negative statement and does not understand that the opposite is intended to be emphasized.

Solution: Render it as an emphatic affirmation.
- Luke 1:37 (NCV) "God *can do anything!"*
- Acts 15:2 (NIV) "This brought Paul and Barnabas into *sharp dispute and debate* with them."
  (TEV) "Paul and Barnabas *got into a fierce argument* with them about this." (Similarly REB.)
  (NLT) "Paul and Barnabas disagreeing with them, *argued forcefully and at length."*
  (NET) "Paul and Barnabas had *a major argument and debate* with them."
  (ISV) "Paul and Barnabas had *quite a dispute and argument* with them."
- Acts 20:12 (TEV) "They took the young man home alive and were *greatly* comforted." (Similarly ISV, NET, NCV, NIV, NLT, REB.)
  (CEV) "Then the followers took the young man home alive and were *very* happy."

METAPHOR

METAPHOR —an implied comparison of two generally unlike things or events based upon a point of similarity, whether explicit or implied. A metaphor may be direct, with the verb "to be" ("the Lord is a strong tower"), or indirect ("I have finished the race").
- Mark 1:3 (NRSV) *"Prepare the way* of the Lord."
- Acts 2:20 (NIV) "and the moon [*will be turned*] *to blood."*
- Colossians 2:3 (NRSV) "in whom *are hidden all the treasures* of wisdom and knowledge."
- James 1:12 (NIV) "he will *receive the crown of life."*
- James 3:6 (NRSV) "the tongue *is a fire."*
- 1 Peter 1:13 (KJV) *"gird up the loins* of your mind."

Problems: (1) The reader of the translation does not recognize that the expression is figurative and takes the statement literally. (2) The reader recognizes that the statement is not to be taken literally, but does not properly relate the figurative expression with its intended meaning.

Solutions: Check with various speakers of the receptor language to determine if failure to understand the metaphor is a general problem. Readers must understand that a comparison is intended and must know what the point of similarity is. If most have a problem in understanding the metaphor, try filling in parts of the comparison to see how much must be made explicit before it is understood correctly. The less that has to be filled in, the better, since the impact of metaphors will be lost if everything has to be made explicit.

1. Indicate that a comparison is intended by changing the metaphor to a simile with the addition of "like" or "as."
   - Acts 2:20 "and the moon shall become *like* blood."
   - James 3:6 (NCV) "And the tongue is *like* a fire." (Similarly CEV, TEV.)

2. Make explicit the various parts of the topic, image, and points of similarity until the comparison is understood correctly. When the point of similarity is made explicit, a word or phrase must be used that collocates with both the nonfigurative topic and the image with which the topic is being compared.
   - Mark 1:3 "People *prepare* the roads so that they will *be ready* for a king when he comes. In the same way, you must *prepare* your lives so as to *be ready* for the Lord when he comes."
   - Acts 2:20 (TEV) "and the moon will turn *red as* blood." (Similarly CEV, NCV.)
   (NLT) "and the moon will turn *bloodred*."
   - Colossians 2:3 "Christ is the one from whom we *receive* wisdom and knowledge, just as someone *would receive* treasure from a treasure house."
   - James 3:6 "what we say *ruins* things like a fire *ruins* things."
   - James 1:12 "just as an athlete is *rewarded* with a crown, so he will be *rewarded* with eternal life."
   - 1 Peter 1:13 "As a man *prepares for action* by girding up the tunic around his loins, so you must *prepare* your minds *for action*."

METAPHOR

3. Use a comparison with the same point of similarity that is meaningful in the receptor language.
   📖 James 1:12 "he will win the *gold medal* of life."
4. Translate without the comparison if (a) the metaphor already exists in the receptor language with a different meaning, (b) the image involves unknown objects that would require explanations, (c) the point of similarity is not regarded as similar in the receptor language, or (d) filling out all the details would result in a cumbersome and stylistically heavy translation, losing the beauty of a metaphor.
   📖 Mark 1:3 "*Get ready* for when the Lord comes."
   📖 Acts 2:20 "and the moon will *turn ominously red.*"
   📖 Colossians 2:3 "Christ is *the source* of wisdom and knowledge for us."
   📖 James 1:12 (NCV) "God will *reward* them with life forever." (Similarly CEV.)
   (NRSV) "he will *receive in reward* the life which God has promised." (Similarly (TEV.)
   📖 James 3:6 "what we say *ruins things.*"
   📖 1 Peter 1:13 (NIV) "*prepare* your minds for action." (Similarly ISV, NET, NRSV, TEV.)
   (NCV) "*prepare* your minds for service."
   (NLT) "*think clearly.*"
   (CEV) "*be alert.*"

However, the comparison needs to be kept in spite of difficulties if (a) the listener in the story itself misunderstands it (e.g., the meaning of leaven in Mark 8:15), (b) if Christians are divided on whether it is figurative or literal (e.g., the bread being Christ's body in Matt. 26:26), (c) if the figure is extended and gives details about the figurative elements (e.g., building on the foundation and having the material tested by fire in 1 Cor. 3:12), or (d) if the figure has a symbolic function (e.g., the sacrificial lamb in John 1:29).

MISCELLANEOUS —a catch-all category for any entry that does not fit in any of the other categories. Each language will have other problems in translation not covered by the categories in this book.

NATURALNESS IN TRANSLATION —the use of language forms that correspond to actual usage of the receptor language and are considered normal speech by mother-tongue speakers of the receptor language.

Problems:
1. When the translation is not natural, it is not idiomatic and often the meaning of the original message is obscured or changed. Readers are discouraged because reading is difficult and they do not enjoy it.
   - 2 Corinthians 1:12 (KJV) "For our rejoicing is this, the testimony of our conscience, that in simplicity and godly sincerity, not with fleshly wisdom, but by the grace of God, we have had our conversation in the world, and more abundantly to youward."

   Solution: Conform the translation to the patterns of the receptor language. Use native speaker's reactions, naturalness counts, and discourse analysis.
   - 2 Corinthians 1:12 (TEV) "We are proud that our conscience assures us that our lives in this world, and especially our relations with you, have been ruled by God-given frankness and sincerity, by the power of God's grace and not by human wisdom."
   (NLT) "We can say with confidence and a clear conscience that we have been honest and sincere in all our dealings. We have depended on God's grace, not on our own earthly wisdom. That is how we have acted toward everyone, and especially toward you."

2. Trying to keep the same length and structure violates good style in the receptor language.
   - 2 Thessalonians 1:3-10 is one sentence in Greek and in KJV.

   Solution: Break up the sentences to the normal length of sentences for the type of discourse involved. Change the order of embedded clauses or make them separate sentences.
   - 2 Thessalonians 1:3-10 is 5 sentences in NRSV, 6 sentences in LB, NET, and REB, 7 sentences in ISV, 8 sentences in NIV and NLT, 9 sentences in TEV, 10 sentences in CEV, and 15 sentences in NCV.

NEGATION —a grammatical marker that indicates denial, prohibition, or refusal. Whole propositions or only certain parts of a proposition may be negated. Double negatives may occur. In Greek, there are

two forms of negation in questions, one expecting a positive answer (*ou*) and the other assuming a negative response (*mē*).
- Matthew 5:17 (NIV) "I have not come to abolish them but to fulfill them."
- Matthew 13:57 (KJV) "A prophet is not without honour, save in his own country, and in his own house."
- Mark 4:22 (NRSV) "For there is nothing hidden, except to be disclosed."
- Mark 4:34 (NIV) "He did not say anything to them without using a parable."
- John 4:35 (NIV) ""Do you not [*ou*] say, 'Four months more and then harvest'?"
- John 14:6 (NIV) "No one comes to the Father except through me."
- John 7:41 "Shall not [*mē*] Christ come out of Galilee?"

Problem: The negative confuses the reader or even comes out negating the wrong portion of the proposition.

Solutions:
1. Change negative statements to positive statements.
   - Matthew 13:57 (NLT) "A prophet is honored everywhere except in his own hometown and among his own family." (Similarly NCV, TEV.)
   - Mark 4:22 (TEV) "Whatever is hidden away will be brought out into the open." (Similarly NCV, NIV, NLT.)
   - Mark 4:34 (NCV) "He always used stories to teach them."
   - John 4:35 (ISV) "You say, don't you, 'In four more months the harvest will be here?'" (Similarly NET, NRSV, REB.)
     (NCV) "You have a saying, 'Four more months till harvest.'"
     (CEV) "You may say that there are still four months until harvest time."
   - John 7:41 (ISV) "The Christ doesn't come from Galilee, does he?" (Similarly NET, NRSV.)
     (REB) "Surely the Messiah is not to come from Galilee."
     (NCV) "The Christ will not come from Galilee."

2. Restate the proposition so that the word "only" carries the negative meaning.
   - Matthew 13:57 (ISV) "A prophet is without honor *only* in his hometown and in his own home."
   - Mark 4:34 (NLT) "In fact, in his public teaching he taught *only* with parables."
   - John 14:6 (NCV) "The *only* way to the Father is through me."

3. Put the verb with the positive part of the statement.
   📖 Matthew 5:17 "I have come to fulfill them, not to abolish them."

NUMBERING —the identification of chapters and verses in the Bible by numbers. Sometimes they disrupt the discourse. Notes relating to different chapter-verse numbering traditions should also be included in this category.

Problems:
1. The translator does not know the factors to consider for adopting a numbering system.

   Solution: The numbers should appear to be distinct from the text and prominent enough to find them on the page. Yet they should not intrude into the smooth reading of the text in paragraphs. Numbers can be made somewhat unobtrusive by raising them and making them smaller than the regular text characters. Some translators keep the numbers on the line of the text and make them bold them to make them both distinct and easy to find. There are two systems for chapter-verse numbering: separating chapter and verse by a colon or by a period, that is, 12:36 or 12.36. The system used in national language versions should be followed unless there are other factors to be considered.

2. The numbering system of familiar versions has carried over into the translation.

   Solution: Roman numerals are an unnecessary complication. Instead of I Kings and II Kings, it would be easier for new readers to see 1 Kings and 2 Kings. Introductory material before the first book does not need to have Roman numerals for page numbers. TEV and CEV do not number those pages. NET begins regular numbering from the title page.

OLD TESTAMENT QUOTATION —the citation of an Old Testament passage in the New Testament text. The quotation may be virtually word for word or it may give the general sense of the passage.

New Testament authors may sometimes apply an OT text in a way that seems rather different from its meaning in the OT context. The source of the quotation may be the Hebrew OT or the Septuagint, the ancient Greek translation of the OT which, in some passages, is a quite free rendering of the Hebrew text. The NT contains over 380 direct

OLD TESTAMENT QUOTATION

quotations from the OT. Almost 70 of these are clearly based on the Septuagint translation. Besides the direct quotations, there are many hundreds of NT passages that have allusions or verbal parallels to the OT.

📖 Deuteronomy 21:23 (NRSV) "anyone hung on a tree is under God's curse."; Galatians 3:13 (NRSV) "it is written, 'Cursed is everyone who hangs on a tree.'"

Problems:
1. Translators sometimes change the meaning of the NT text in order to conform to the OT passage.
    📖 Deuteronomy 21:23 (REB) "Anyone who is hanged is accursed in the sight of God."; Galatians 3:13 (REB) "for scripture says, 'Cursed is everyone who is hanged on a gibbet.'"

2. The NT translation changes the wording of the quotation from the wording of the OT passage when they are both identical in meaning.
    📖 Deuteronomy 21:23 (TEV) "a dead body hanging on a post brings God's curse on the land."; Galatians 3:13 (TEV) "the scripture says, 'Anyone who is hanged on a tree is under God's curse.'"

Solution: Translate the meaning of the Greek text of the NT as it stands. The quotation may be intended to give only the sense of the OT passage and not be a word-for-word quotation. When it is clear that the Greek form is an exact translation of the Hebrew, endeavor to use the same wording in both Testaments. In translating prophecies, be careful to translate in a way that includes meanings that the OT text allowed and that is also consistent with the intention of the NT text.

📖 Deuteronomy 21:23 (NCV) "anyone whose body is displayed on a tree is cursed by God."; Galatians 3:13 (NCV) "It is written in the Scriptures, 'Anyone whose body is displayed on a tree is cursed." Footnote: "Deuteronomy 21:22-23 says that when a person was killed for doing wrong, the body was hung on a tree to show shame. Paul means that the cross of Jesus was like that."

📖 Deuteronomy 21:23 (NIV) "anyone who is hung on a tree is under God's curse." *The NIV Study Bible* footnote: "The offender was first put to death, then 'hung on a tree' ... or, as the Hebrew for this phrase doubtless intends, 'impaled on a pole'"; Galatians 3:13 (NIV) "it is written: 'Cursed is everyone who is hung on a tree.'" *The NIV Study Bible* footnote: "*tree.*

Used in classical Greek of stocks and poles on which bodies were impaled, here of the cross."

OMISSION OF INFORMATION IN TRANSLATION —the loss of information included in the source text.

Problem: Explicit or implicit information in the source language that is necessary for communicating the meaning is lacking.
> 1 John 1:9 (CEV) "But if we confess our sins to God, he can always be trusted to forgive us and take our sins away.'

Solution: Include the information.
> 1 John 1:9 (TEV) "But if we confess our sins to God, he will keep his promise *and do what is right*: he will forgive our sins and purify us from all wrongdoing."

ORTHOGRAPHY ISSUES —all that pertains to the spelling system used in the translation. It includes rules of capitalization, punctuation, and word breaks.

Problems:
1. The translator has not decided whether or not to capitalize words such Gentile/gentile, Temple/temple, Lord/lord, or is inconsistent in doing so.

   Solution: Generally, a title would be capitalized and a descriptive word would be in lower case. Whatever system is adopted, it should be consistently applied.

2. There is a question about how closely the national language orthography should be followed. For instance, should a more phonetic letter be used, such as *k* for the national language *qu* and *w* for *ou*?

   Solution: In many locations, people have learned to read and understand the national language and it would be helpful to use the same orthography for the same sounds. Yet a simpler system is easier to teach new readers. The translator should consult literacy experts and gain experience in teaching reading. For users of the translation who have learned to read in the national language but have not yet learned to read in their own language, an explanation in the national language concerning the letters used in the translation may be enough to enable them to read the translation.

OTHER GRAMMATICAL RELATIONSHIPS (within a clause or proposition) —relationships between words or phrases within a clause or proposition. This includes all lower-level grammatical relationships except for those that are separately labeled.

Problems:
1. The clause, sentence, or paragraph in the translation does not develop the theme of the paragraph or support another clause as the Greek text does.

   Solution: Determine the relationship involved (the *Semantic and Structural Analysis* series focuses on such relationships). Then indicate the relationship in the way the receptor language normally does.

2. The order of related units in Greek is different from the normal order in the receptor language. A language may always have negative clauses precede positive clauses. Background information may always come before the main action of a narrative. A language may require the reason clause to follow the result clause to be effective.
   📖 2 Corinthians 4:13 (NIV) "I believed, therefore I have spoken."

   Solution: Follow the order that speakers of the receptor language find natural.
   📖 2 Corinthians 4:13 (CEV) "I spoke because I had faith."
   (Similarly TEV.)

PARABLE AND ALLEGORY —a short story that is used to illustrate a spiritual truth or principle (parable); an extended simile or metaphor (allegory).

Problem: The implied comparison in the parable is not apparent.
📖 Matthew 13:24 (NIV) "The kingdom of heaven *is like a man* who sowed some seed in his field."

Solution: Make it clear that the comparison is to the whole situation.
📖 Matthew 13:24 (CEV) "The kingdom of heaven *is like what happened when* a farmer scattered good seed in a field."
(TEV) "The kingdom of heaven *is like this*. A man sowed good seed in his field."

PARALLEL PASSAGE —reference to another unit of text, often a passage in a different book of the Bible, that describes the same incident or one which is identical or very similar in content.

Problems:
1. Passages that are identical or similar in the source language have been translated independently and are not worded the same or similarly in the receptor language.

   Solution: The translation should reflect the similarities (and differences) between the parallel passages. By giving a parallel reference, the reader is invited to compare them.

2. Passages that are parallel seem to contradict each other in some important way.
   - 1 Kings 4:26 (TEV) "Solomon had *forty thousand stalls* for his chariot horses and twelve thousand cavalry horses." Reference "2 Ch 9:25."
   - 2 Chronicles 9:25 (TEV) "King Solomon also had *four thousand stalls* for his chariots and horses, and had twelve thousand cavalry horses." Reference: "1 K 4:26."

   Solution: Even though it might be conjectured that the figure *forty thousand* was a copyist error, a translation must keep the contradictory wording.

3. The parallel reference is more puzzling than helpful. For example, CEV and TEV list John 2:13-22 as parallel with Matthew 21:12-13, Mark 11:15-17, and Luke 19:45-46. However, the incident in John comes just after Jesus began his ministry but the time in the other Gospels is in the final week of Jesus' life.

   Solution: If there is a reasonable doubt about the incidents referring to the same event, it is better not to include a cross-reference which may confuse readers even if the events are similar.

PARALLELISM

—the occurrence of two or more items whose meanings are either partially or totally the same. The repetition is often used for highlighting, emphasis, and poetic effects.

a. *Syntactic.* This occurs when the meaning of one proposition is expressed by a second proposition in different words, sometimes in a slightly modified form. This type of parallelism is commonly found in Hebrew poetry (see equivalence parallelism under POETRY).
   - Matthew 11:30 (NIV) "For my yoke is easy and my burden is light."
   - James 4:8 (NIV) "Wash your hands, you sinners, and purify your hearts, you double-minded."

PARALLELISM

b. *Lexical.* This occurs when two lexical items form a doublet. The first term may be repeated with an identical term or with an almost synonymous term which adds little further meaning. Some doublets may form generic-specific pairs, positive-negative pairs, or literal-figurative pairs.

- Luke 10:41 (NRSV) "Martha, Martha."
- John 3:3 (KJV) "Verily, verily."
- Matthew 5:12 (NRSV) *"Rejoice* and *be glad."*
- Matthew 3:15 (KJV) *"answering said."*
- Romans 2:8 (NRSV) "there will be *wrath* and *fury."*
- Mark 2:25 (KJV) "he *had need,* and *was ahungered."*
- Acts 18:9 (NRSV) *"speak* and *do not be silent."*
- 1 Corinthians 15:52 (NRSV) "in *a moment,* in *the twinkling of an eye."*

Problems:

1. It is difficult to feature the parallelism of the two propositions.

   Solution: Translate the meaning plainly even if the parallelism is not prominent in the translation.
   - Matthew 11:30 (NLT) "For my yoke fits perfectly, and the burden I give you is light."
     (NCV) "The teaching that I ask you to accept is easy; the load I give you to carry is light."
   - James 4:8 (NCV) "You sinners, clean sin out of your lives. You who are trying to follow God and the world at the same time, make your thinking pure."

2. Repetition sounds unnatural in the receptor language or a wrong connotation is communicated, e.g., repeating a person's name may indicate jeering in the receptor language.

   Solution: Use the term only once and indicate the function of the repetition in a way that is natural in the receptor language.
   - Luke 10:41 (LB) "Martha, dear friend."
     (NLT) "My dear Martha."
   - John 3:3 (NIV) "I tell you the truth." (Similarly NCV, TEV.)
     (NET) "I tell you the solemn truth."
     (CEV) "I tell you for certain."
     (NLT) "I assure you."
     (NRSV) "Very truly, I tell you."
     (REB) "In very truth I tell you."

3. The receptor language does not normally join synonyms to intensify a word or the receptor language does not have synonyms for the meaning.

   Solution: Use the one term the language has. If it needs to be intensified, do so in the manner that the language does, e.g., using intensifier words such as "very much" or "greatly."
   - Matthew 3:15 (NIV) "replied." (Also NET, REB.) (NCV) "answered." (Also CEV, ISV, NRSV, TEV.) (NLT) "said."
   - Matthew 5:2 "Greatly rejoice."
   - Romans 2:8 "God will be *very* angry with them."
   - Mark 2:25 (NCV): "he and those with him were hungry and needed food." (NLT) "he and his companions were hungry."
   - Acts 18:9 "keep on preaching."
   - 1 Corinthians 15:52 "it will happen suddenly."

PARTICIPANT REFERENCE —the references to the people involved in an account, whether direct or indirect.

a. *Introduction of a new participant.* Languages have their own ways of introducing participants into a narrative. Some require that all participants be introduced at the beginning. Others allow them to be introduced into the flow of the narrative. There may be special clause types to introduce them. Sometimes there is a difference between the ways major and minor participants are introduced.

   Problem: People suddenly appear without adequate introduction from the viewpoint of the readers of the receptor language.
   - Mark 2:2, 3 (KJV) "... and he preached the word unto them. And *they* came unto him, bringing one sick of the palsy, which was borne of four."

   Solution: Text material must be analyzed to discover the way participants are introduced into an account and this should be followed in the translation.
   - Mark 2:2, 3 (TEV) "Jesus was preaching the message to them when *four men* [interpreting "they" to refer to only the four men] arrived, carrying a paralyzed man to Jesus." (Similarly CEV, NCV, NLT, REB.)
   - Mark 2:2, 3 (NIV) "... and he preached the word to them. *Some men* [interpreting "they" to refer to more than the four

men] came, bringing to him a paralytic, carried by four of them." (Similarly ISV, NET, NRSV.)

b. *Back reference.* Once introduced, there are differences among languages concerning how to refer to the participants. Perhaps a pronoun is used until a noun is needed to avoid confusion about the reference. But some languages might distinguish between participants with proper names, demonstratives, or generic words.

Problem: Readers refer a pronoun to the wrong person or they are uncertain as to whom it refers.
   Mark 1:2 (NRSV) "As it is written in the prophet Isaiah, 'See, *I* am sending my messenger ahead of you.'"
   Mark 9:20–21 (KJV) "And *they* brought *him* unto *him:* and when *he* saw *him*, straightway the spirit tare *him;* and *he* fell on the ground, and wallowed foaming. And *he* asked *his* father, How long is it ago since this came unto *him*?"

Solution: Study the pronoun system of the receptor language and be careful to follow the same pattern. For example, in some languages the main participant is always referred to by pronouns, minor participants by nouns. Often nouns must be used where the source language uses pronouns.
   Mark 1:2 (CEV) "It began just as *God* had said in the book written by Isaiah the prophet, '*I* am sending my messenger to get the way ready for you.'"
   (TEV) "It began as the prophet Isaiah had written: '*God* said, "*I* will send my messenger ahead of you to open the way for you." (Similarly NLT.)
   Mark 9:20–21 (NIV) "So *they* brought *him*. When *the spirit* saw *Jesus, it* immediately threw *the boy* into a convulsion. *He* fell to the ground and rolled around, foaming at the mouth. *Jesus* asked *the boy's* father, 'How long has *he* been like this?'" (Similarly CEV, NCV, NLT, TEV.)

PASSIVE VOICE —a verb form which indicates that the grammatical subject is the person or thing to which the action is done. It differs from the active verb form in that the subject of the active form is the one who does the action. The use of a passive form often puts the focus on the receiver of the action. A passive form may be used when the agent is irrelevant or unknown. It was a Jewish custom to use the passive form in order to avoid using God's name.

PASSIVE VOICE

- Matthew 5:4 (NIV) *"Blessed* are those who mourn, for they *will be comforted."*
- Matthew 7:1 (NIV) "Do not judge, or you too *will be judged."*
- Mark 10:45 (NIV) "For even the Son of Man did not come *to be served,* but to serve."
- Luke 3:21 (NIV) "Jesus *was baptized* too."
- Colossians 1:11 (KJV) *"Strengthened* with *all might."*

Problems: (1) The receptor language does not use passives at all or does not use them frequently. (2) Although passives are normal in the language, the reader does not understand who the implied agent is. (3) Passives in the receptor language may have different functions or emotive meanings than in the source language. For example, in Thai, passives are used to insult people while, in Korean and Japanese, the passives may be used to portray suffering.

Solutions: Determine why the passive was used in the source language and try to achieve the same purpose in the receptor language while using active verbs.

1. There may be a way of keeping the focus on the receiver of the action.
   - Luke 3:21 *"Concerning Jesus,* John baptized him."

2. There may be a non-specific form to use for the agents.
   - Mark 10:45 "For even the Son of Man did not come so that *they/others* might serve him, but so that he might serve them."

3. If avoidance of God's name is not required in the receptor language, it can be supplied.
   - Matthew 5:4 (NLT) *"God blesses* those who mourn, for they will be comforted." (Similarly CEV.)
   (NCV) "Those who are sad now are happy, because *God will comfort* them." (Similarly TEV.)
   - Matthew 7:1 (TEV) "Do not judge others, so that *God* will not judge you." (Similarly CEV.)
   - Colossians 1:11 (NCV) *"God will strengthen* you with his own great power."

PERSONIFICATION —a figure of speech in which inanimate objects or abstract ideas are spoken of as if they had human qualities or form.
- Matthew 11:19 (KJV) "But wisdom is justified of her *children."*
- Romans 13:10 (NIV) "Love does no harm to *its neighbor."*

📖 James 1:15 (NET) "Then when desire *conceives*, it *gives birth* to sin, and when sin is *full grown*, it *brings forth* death."

Problems: (1) The reader of the translation does not recognize that the expression is figurative and takes the statement literally. (2) The reader recognizes that the statement is not to be taken literally, but does not properly relate the figurative expression with its intended meaning.

Solution: Use words that collocate in the receptor language.

📖 Matthew 11:19 (TEV) "God's wisdom, however, is shown to be true by its results." (Similarly REB.)

(NLT) "But wisdom is shown to be right by what results from it."

📖 Romans 13:10 (TEV) "If you love someone, you will never do him wrong."

(CEV) "No one who loves others will harm them."

📖 James 1:15 (NLT) "These evil desires lead to evil actions, and evil actions lead to death."

(CEV) "Our desires make us sin, and when sin is finished with us, it leaves us dead."

PERSPECTIVE/DIRECTION

—the author's point of view as revealed in his choice of words. In many languages, the direction of the action, away from or towards the position of the writer, is a stylistic feature.

📖 John 11:29 (KJV) "As soon as she heard that, she arose quickly, and *came* unto him."

📖 Galatians 1:21 (KJV) "Afterward I *came* into the regions of Syria and Cilicia."

Problem: Some languages might require that the direction be included, e.g., "he *came* doing something," or "he *went* doing something," or "he *rose* doing something." This type of direction indication is used extensively in many languages. Often the direction is oriented in relation to the location of the speaker. If the language being used as a source language does not have this feature, this stylistic device is often ignored, resulting in unnatural translation.

Solution: If frequent use of such verbs is a feature of the receptor language, translators should make a careful study of this feature in natural texts and then check their translations for naturalness. They can experiment with oral drafting or retelling to improve the naturalness of the text.

📖 John 11:29 (CEV) "As soon as Mary heard this, she got up and *went out* to Jesus." (Similarly ISV, NCV, NET, NIV, NLT, NRSV, REB, TEV.)

📖 Galatians 1:21 (NRSV) "Then I *went* into the regions of Syria and Cilicia." (Similarly CEV, ISV, NCV, NET, NIV, NLT, TEV.)

(REB) "Then I *left for* the regions of Syria and Cilicia."

PICTURE SELECTION —the selection of a drawing that illustrates the text or provides background information about the biblical culture. Pictures can acquaint the reader with unknown animals, plants, objects, and activities. In addition, they can be used to stimulate interest in the content of the text. They can illustrate incidents in the narration that will encourage reading of the text to learn more about it. To be useful, pictures must be culturally and historically accurate and selected for the needs of the receptor-language audience.

Problems:
1. The pictures are not understood correctly. Perhaps showing only part of a person does not convey the impression that the rest of the person is outside the picture frame. Perhaps shading is puzzling. Perhaps perspective is not understood.

    Solution: Each picture needs to be tested with the intended audience. Ask questions concerning the picture: what it is about, whether there is something strange about it, etc. It is best to avoid mixing two distinctive styles of pictures. A caption can be included under the picture if it is short and has a different typeface to avoid confusing it with the main text.

2. The picture is not positioned in the best location on the page.

    Solution: Match the shape of the picture with the space available on the page. Horizontal landscape pictures often need text on the same page to fill unused space. Vertical portrait pictures can fill an entire page or be reduced to have text flow around them. Also try to have the direction of motion go toward the center of the book. For example, a person facing to the left should normally appear on a right side (odd-numbered page).

POETRY —a particular genre of speech, distinct from prose. Ideas with a high emotional content are often expressed in poetry form, for example, praise songs or lamentations. Different languages use different forms for poetry, for example, parallelism (as in much biblical poetry), rhyme, rhythm, alliteration, chiasmus, onomatopoeia, acrostic patterns, repetition, and recurrent phrases. Poetry is often characterized by extensive use of figurative language. The use of a special layout may help present the poetic structure.

The outstanding characteristic of biblical poetry is parallelism where two, and sometimes three, lines are connected in some way. Poetry is found in the New Testament in the quotations from Old Testament poetic passages, contemporary Christian hymns (Philippians 2:6–11 and 1 Timothy 3:16), and the songs in Luke (1:46–55, 1:68–79, 2:14, and 2:26–32). There are three typical types of parallelism in Hebrew poetry.

1. *Equivalence parallelism.* The thought of the first line is repeated in the second, using other words that differ very little in meaning. Sometimes one line is a metaphorical expression of the other.
   - Psalm 33:10 (NIV) "The LORD foils the plans of the nations; he thwarts the purposes of the peoples."
   - Isaiah 53:4 (NIV) "Surely he took up our infirmities, and carried our sorrows."

2. *Contrastive parallelism.* The second line gives the opposite of the thought of the first line.
   - Psalm 145:20 (NIV) "The LORD watches over all who love him, but the wicked he will destroy."

3. *Synthetic parallelism.* The second line develops or completes the thought of the first. This is not strictly parallelism, but there may be a Hebrew rhythm and style that keeps it a part of a poetic passage.
   - Psalm 82:8 (NIV) "Rise up, O God, judge the earth, for all the nations are your inheritance."

Problem: The reader does not realize that the translation contains a poetic passage.

Solutions:
1. Use a poetry format to set the poetry apart from the rest of the text. This can be done by indenting the whole poetic passage and having each line of poetry begin a new line of text.
   - Psalm 33:10–11 (NIV)
      "The Lord foils the plans of the nations;
         he thwarts the purposes of the peoples.
      But the plans of the Lord stand firm forever,
         the purposes of his heart through all generations."

2. Parallelism can be duplicated in a translation, but poetry in the NT that does not use parallelism could be indicated by using a poetry form of the receptor language. Rhyming occurs in English and could be used in an English translation if it does not distort the meaning.
   📖 Titus 1:12 (ISV) "One of their very own prophets said,
   'Liars ever, men of Crete,
   Savage brutes that live to eat.'"

3. Perhaps the quotation should be translated as regular prose. In an expository passage where a statement from the Old Testament is used in the argument, it may not seem appropriate to set the quotation apart from the rest of the text.
   📖 Romans 12:19 (ISV) "Don't take revenge, dear friends. Instead, leave room for God's wrath. For it is written, 'Vengeance belongs to me. I will pay them back, says the Lord.'" (Similarly ISV, NCV, NET, NIV, NRSV, REB, TEV.)

PROMINENCE —the use of discourse features to make parts of the material more important than other parts. Prominence is concerned with the focus of a passage or the emphasis of some part of it. Often this is indicated by word order, repetition, figures of speech, or phrases that direct attention to the item. Peak, foregrounding, and backgrounding are involved in the way material is presented.

Problems:
1. In an effort to achieve a clear translation, the translator fills out each ellipsis, breaks the sentences into short unrelated units, and generally restructures the message so that the focus of the original is lost.

   Solution: The meaning of the source text must be carefully studied. The theme of each paragraph and the focus of each sentence should be kept in the translation.

2. The focus of a unit is not carried through into the translation.
   📖 Matthew 16:15 (CEV) "But who do you say I am?" (Greek makes "you" prominent).

   Solution: Use the resources of the language to direct the focus on the proper element.
   📖 Matthew 16:15 (NIV): "*'But what about you?'* he asked. *'Who do you say I am?'*" (Similarly REB, TEV.)

PRONOMINAL REFERENCE —referring to a previously mentioned or implicitly understood person, place, thing, or event by the use of a pronoun.

a. *Extended use.* In extended use, the stated person and number of the pronoun do not agree with who is actually referred to.
   (1) *I* may also mean "we," "anyone," or "everyone."
      📖 1 Corinthians 13:1 (NRSV) "If *I* [= we/anyone] speak in the tongues of mortals and of angels."
   (2) *We* may mean "I."
      📖 Hebrews 2:5 (NRSV) "... the coming world, about which *we* [= I] are speaking."
   (3) *You* (singular) may mean "you all," "anyone," or "everyone."
      📖 1 Corinthians 4:7 (NRSV) "For who sees anything different in *you* [singular = plural]?"
      📖 Matthew 6:2-4, 6, 17-18, 21-23 have "you (singular)" and 6:1, 5, 7-16, 19-20, 25, 27-34 have "you (plural)" without any apparent difference of meaning.
   (4) *He* may mean "they," "you," "anyone," or "I."
      📖 John 4:10 (NRSV) "you would have asked *him* [= me], and *he* [= I] would have given you living water."
   (5) *They* may mean "you all" or "he."
      📖 Matthew 2:20 (NRSV) "for *those* [= he] who were seeking the child's life are dead."

   Problem: The reader does not recognize the extended usage of the pronouns.

   Solution: Translate according to the way the receptor language indicates the intended reference.

b. *Dual-plural.* Some languages have three categories of number for pronouns and verbs: singular, dual, and plural. But Greek, like most languages, distinguishes only between singular and plural.

   Problem: The receptor language requires that forms for "we" and "us" specify whether the number is dual or plural.
      📖 Colossians 1:9 (NRSV) "For this reason, since the day *we* heard it, *we* have not ceased praying for you." [Does "we" refer to Paul and Timothy (1:1) or to Paul and all the Christians mentioned in chapter 4, or is it an editorial "we" referring to Paul alone?]

   Solution: Study the context, consider what the commentaries say, and decide what fits the context best.

📖 Colossians 1:9 "For this reason, since the day *we (dual)* heard it, *we (dual)* have not ceased praying for you."

c. *Inclusive/exclusive first person plural.* Some languages require that forms for *we, our,* and *us* specify whether it includes or excludes the person or persons addressed. Greek does not show this distinction.

Problem: The receptor language grammar requires that the inclusive/exclusive distinction be shown.

📖 Luke 7:4b–4 (NIV) "This man deserves to have you do this, because he loves *our* nation and has built *our* synagogue."

📖 John 4:12 (NIV) "Are you greater than *our* father Jacob, who gave *us* the well?"

Solution: Study the context, consider what the commentaries say, and decide what fits the context best.

📖 Luke 7:4b–4 "This man deserves to have you do this, because he loves *our (inclusive)* nation and his built *our (exclusive)* synagogue."

📖 John 4:12 "Are you greater than *our (inclusive)* ancestor Jacob who gave *us (exclusive)* the well?"

d. *Implied exclusion.* When stating something is true for those referred to by the person of the pronoun or verb, it may be implied in some languages that this is not true for anyone other than those referred to. Other languages leave this open.

Problem: The receptor language gives the wrong implications in the translation.

📖 Matthew 5:16 "*your* Father in heaven" would imply that God is not Jesus' Father.

📖 Acts 2:15 "*these men* are not drunk" would imply that Peter was drunk.

📖 Philippians 4:13 (NRSV) "*I* can do all things through him who strengthens me" would imply that the Philippians cannot do so.

Solution: Include all those for whom the statement is true.

📖 Matthew 5:16 "*our* Father who is in heaven."

📖 Acts 2:15 "*we* are not drunk."

📖 Philippians 4:13 "*We* can do all things through him who strengthens us."

e. *Pronoun system mismatch.* Some languages have other systems that do not have equivalents in the biblical pronoun system. There might be separate sets of pronouns determined by the shapes and sizes of the objects they refer to. There might be different pronouns used according to the importance and rank of the person referred to. There might be an indefinite third person pronoun. These all require the translator to make a decision about which form to use in harmony with the context.

f. *Gender appropriateness.* In some languages, notably English, the masculine forms of pronouns are used in contexts where the reference is to anyone, whether a man or a woman. In this case, and where the reference in the original text is to both men and women, the rendering in the translation should be such that the same meaning will be understood by the audience.
 📖 Romans 10:1 (NIV) "Brothers"
 📖 Romans 10:10 (KJV) "For with the heart *man* believeth unto righteousness."
 📖 1 Timothy 2:4 (NIV) "who wants *all men* to be saved."

Problem: The receptor language assumes that women are not included.

Solution: Make explicit that both men and women are intended.
 📖 Romans 10:1 (NCV) "Brothers and sisters." (Also NET, NLT, NRSV.)
 (REB) "Friends" (Similarly CEV, TEV.)
 📖 Romans 10:10 (NRSV) "For *one* believes with the heart and so is justified." (Similarly NET.)
 (ISV) "For *a person* believes with *his* heart and is justified."
 (NLT) "For it is by believing in *your* heart that *you* are made right with God." (Similarly CEV, NIV.)
 (TEV) "For it is by *our* faith that *we* are put right with God." (Similarly NCV.)
 (REB) "For faith in the heart leads to righteousness."
 📖 1 Timothy 2:4 (NCV) "who wants *all people* to be saved." (Similarly NET.)
 (NLT) "he wants *everyone* to be saved." (Similarly CEV, ISV, NRSV, TEV.)
 (REB) "whose will it is that *all* should find salvation."

PROPER NAME —names in the Bible are often transliterated from a major language or from the original biblical language.

Problems:
1. The name of a person or object is spelled differently in different books.
   - Acts 18:2 (KJV) "and with him *Priscilla* and Aquila." 2 Timothy 4:19 (KJV) "Salute *Prisca* and Aquila."

   Solution: Once that it is determined that both spellings of a name refer to the same individual with no significant difference in the spelling, translation of both names can use in the same spelling to avoid confusion. A change of name from "Abram" to "Abraham is significant and the different spellings must be kept.
   - 2 Timothy 4:19 (NIV) "Greet *Priscilla* and Aquila." (Similarly CEV, NCV, NLT, TEV.)
   - (ISV) "Greet *Prisca* and Aquila." Footnote: "I.e. Priscilla."
   - Genesis 17:5 (TEV) "Your name will no longer be *Abram*, but *Abraham*."

2. The same person or object has two names and it is likely that the reader will not know that one of the names refers to the same person or object that is better known by the other name.
   - Exodus 3:1 (NIV) "he led the flock to the far side of the desert and came to *Horeb*, the mountain of God."
   - Acts 7:45 (KJV) "which also our fathers that came after brought in with *Jesus*."
   - Galatians 2:11 (NRSV) "But when *Cephas* came to Antioch, I opposed him to his face."

   Solution: Use the better known name. A footnote may be attached to show that it is not a mistranslation.
   - Exodus 3:1 (TEV) "he led the flock across the desert and came to *Sinai*, the holy mountain." (Similarly CEV, NLT.)
   - Acts 7:45 (CEV) "Later it was given to our ancestors, and they took it with them when they went with *Joshua*." (Similarly ISV, NET, NIV, NRSV, REB, TEV.)
   - Galatians 2:11 (NIV) "When *Peter* came to Antioch, I opposed him to his face." Footnote: "Greek *Cephas*." (Similarly CEV, NCV, NLT, TEV.)

3. The meaning of a person's name is significant.
   - Matthew 1:21 (CEV) "Then after her baby is born, name him *Jesus*—because he will save his people from their sins."

Solution: Attach a footnote to explain the meaning of the name.
- Matthew 1:21 (CEV) Footnote: "In Hebrew the name 'Jesus' means 'the Lord saves.'" (Similarly ISV, NCV, NET, NIV, NLT, REB.)

4. Different people have the same name.
   - Matthew 2:1 (CEV) "When Jesus was born in the village of Bethlehem in Judea, *Herod* was king."
   - Matthew 14:1 (CEV) "About this time *Herod* the ruler heard the news about Jesus."

   Solution: Attach a footnote to explain which person is being referred to.
   - Matthew 14:1 (CEV) Footnote: "*Herod the ruler:* Herod Antipas, the son of Herod the Great (2.1)." (Similarly ISV, NLT.)

5. The translation does not distinguish between a title and a proper name.
   - Mark 8:29 (NCV) "Peter answered, 'You are *the Christ.*'"
   - Hebrews 11:24 (NIV) "By faith Moses, when he had grown up, refused to be known as the son of *Pharaoh's* daughter."

   Solution: "Christ" often occurs as another name for Jesus, but in some contexts, especially when accompanied with an article, "the Christ," it is a title meaning the one anointed to rule. There were many Pharaohs, a title of the rulers in Egypt. When a title, translate to show its function.
   - Mark 8:29 (LNT) "Peter replied, 'You are *the Messiah.*'" (Similarly CEV, NRSV, REB, TEV.)
   - Hebrews 11:24 (TEV) "It was faith that made Moses, when he had grown up, refuse to be called the son of *the king's* daughter." (Similarly NCV.)

RELATIONSHIP BETWEEN PROPOSITIONS —the semantic relationships between propositions, such as chronological relationship, restatement (e.g., generic-specific, negative-positive), clarification (e.g., nucleus-comparison, nucleus-manner), logic (e.g., result-reason, means-purpose, condition-consequence), and others. Relationships between propositions may be signaled by relational words (e.g., *and, but, if, because, therefore*), by the form of the verbs, or by other grammatical or semantic features.

Problem: Whereas Greek and many languages have many connective words, some languages have only a few. A Greek paragraph often has a theme proposition with supporting propositions connected by conjunctions. In other languages the relationships may be expressed in other ways.

Solution: Translators should read recent studies on the exact significance of Greek connectives for better understanding of the original meaning. They should also study natural texts in the receptor language in order to understand how relationships expressed in the Greek text are expressed in the receptor language.

RELATIVE CLAUSE
—a clause that is embedded in a sentence to make a comment about a noun. In some languages the clause may often begin with a relative pronoun.

- 📖 Philippians 1:6 (TEV) "And so I am sure that God, *who began this good work in you*, will carry it on until it is finished on the Day of Christ Jesus."
- 📖 Hebrews 13:20-21 (NRSV) "Now may the God of peace, *who brought back from the dead our Lord Jesus, the great shepherd of the sheep, by the blood of the eternal covenant*, make you complete in everything good."

Problems: (1) The receptor language does not have equivalent relative clauses. (2) The relative clause is complicated by event words, unknown objects, or figurative language so that each clause must be translated as a complete sentence.

Solution: The function of the clause must be determined. Then it can be stated as a complete sentence before or after the sentence in which it was embedded.
  - 📖 Philippians 1:6 (CEV) "God is the one who began this good work in you, and I am certain that he won't stop before it is complete on the day that Christ Jesus returns." (Similarly NCV.)
  - 📖 Hebrews 13:20-21 (TEV) "God has raised from death our Lord Jesus, who is the Great Shepherd of the sheep as the result of his sacrificial death, by which the eternal covenant is sealed. May the God of peace provide you with every good thing."

REPETITION
—a redundant expression in which information is explicit more than once in the immediate context and is not necessary for understanding. Repetition may be used for rhetorical effect or emotive impact.

📖 2 Kings 6:17 (KJV) "And Elisha *prayed, and said.*"
📖 Galatians 1:12 (NIV) "*I did not receive it from any man,* nor *was I taught it*; rather, I received it by revelation from Jesus Christ."

Problem: The repetition is not good style in the receptor language.

Solution: Leave out the redundancy.
  📖 2 Kings 6:17 "Then Elisha *prayed.*" (Similarly CEV, REB, TEV.)
  📖 Galatians 1:12 (NLT) "For message came by a direct revelation from Jesus Christ himself. *No one else taught me.*"

RHETORICAL QUESTION —a question that does not expect an answer. The function of a rhetorical question is discovered from the context.

1. It may emphasize a fact that is obviously true.
   📖 Mark 2:7 (NRSV) "Who can forgive sins but God alone?"
   📖 Luke 22:71 (NRSV) "What further testimony do we need? We have heard it ourselves from his own lips!"

2. It may focus on a particular condition.
   📖 James 5:13 (NRSV) "Are any among you suffering? They should pray."

3. It may direct attention to a new topic, a new aspect of a topic, or a conclusion.
   📖 Romans 11:7 (NRSV) "What then?"

4. It may express surprise and amazement.
   📖 Mark 6:2 (NRSV) "Where did this man get all this?"

5. It may express disapproval, rebuke, or prohibition.
   📖 Mark 14:6 (NRSV) "why do you trouble her?"

6. It may express uncertainty.
   📖 Matt. 12:23 (NRSV) "Can this be the Son of David?"

7. It may express exhortation.
   📖 Mark 4:40 (NRSV) "Why are you afraid? Have you still no faith?"

Problems: (1) A rhetorical question is taken as a real question. (2) It is recognized to be a rhetorical question, but it is interpreted differently than what was intended in the source language.

Solutions: Determine the purpose of the rhetorical question and then translate it that way in the receptor language. It may or may not be appropriate to retain the question form.

1. If the question form is retained, check whether some adjustments are needed. It might be proper to provide an answer or change its form.
    - Matthew 12:23 (ISV) "This man isn't the Son of David, *is he?*"
    - Mark 14:6 (ISV) *"Why should* you trouble her?"
    - Luke 22:71 "What further testimony do we need? *None*, because we have heard it ourselves from his own lips!"
    (NIV) *"Why* do we need any more testimony? We have heard it from his own lips." (Similarly ISV, NET.)

2. Translate as a statement, keeping the same emotive quality.
    - Matt. 12:23 (LB) *"Maybe* Jesus is the Messiah!"
    (NCV) *"Perhaps* this man is the son of David."
    - Mark 2:7 (TEV) "God is *the only one who can* forgive sins!"
    (Similarly CEV, NCV.)
    - Mark 4:40 "You *shouldn't be* afraid. *Have* faith!"
    - Mark 6:2 "This man is an amazing man to have gotten all of this!"
    - Mark 14:6 *"Do not* trouble her!"
    - Luke 22:71 (TEV) "We *don't need* any witnesses! We ourselves have heard what he said!"
    - Romans 11:7 (NLT) "So this is the situation."
    (CEV) "This means that . . ."
    (NCV) "So this is what happened."
    - James 5:13 (CEV) *"If you are having* trouble, you should pray."
    (NCV) "Anyone *who is having* troubles should pray."

SECTION HEADING

—a title inserted into the text to divide it into meaningful units. Section headings identify the topic or theme of the following unit of text. They make it easy to locate passages and they encourage people to read complete semantic units, breaking the text at the appropriate places in the larger discourse.

Problems:
1. The grammar of the section heading confuses the readers.

    Solutions: Reader's reactions should be tested to discover what seems most meaningful to them. Perhaps oral stories are known by titles, or contact with the national language has imparted the concept of headings.

1. The form of the heading should be tested to see what is considered proper. It might be a statement of the topic without a verb or it might be a theme statement in sentence form.
   📖 Acts 4:23-31 (NIV) "The Believers' Prayer."
   📖 Acts 4:23-31 (TEV) "The Believers Pray for Boldness."

2. The tense of any verbs in the heading should be tested to see what is considered proper. In some languages the heading should normally be in the present tense. In other languages they should normally be in the past tense.
   📖 Acts 4:23-31 (TEV) "The Believers *Pray* for Boldness."
   📖 Acts 4:23-31 "The Believers *Prayed* for Boldness."

2. The readers consider the heading to be part of the text and get the sequence mixed up.
   📖 Mark 8:1-10 may have the heading "Jesus Feeds Four Thousand People." The reading of the heading and then the following text might cause the readers to think that there were two different occasions of feeding four thousand people.

   Solution: The functions of the headings need to be taught to new readers. Headings should be set off from the body of the text. This may be done by using a different type style, such as italic or boldface letters, a different size type, and centering the headings.

3. The placement of the heading confuses the readers. Section headings dividing up a single event might cause the readers to think that the different sections took place at different times and perhaps involved different people.
   📖 Matthew. 10:1-42 in the TEV is divided into seven sections, each with a heading, although it is reporting only one occasion when Jesus instructed the twelve apostles.

   Solution: Test the translation with various people to see if most are confused. If so, use headings only between distinct events.
   📖 Matthew 10:1-42 is a single section in NIV.

SIMILE —an explicitly stated comparison of two generally unlike things or events based upon an explicit or implied point of comparison. The words "like" or "as" are used in a simile; hence the sense of collocational clash that there is in a metaphor is absent. The point of similarity may not be immediately apparent, just as in a metaphor.

📖 Acts 6:15 (NIV) "they saw that his face was *like* the face of an angel."

📖 1 Peter 1:24 (NIV) "All men are *like* grass."

📖 Revelation 3:3 (NCV) "I will come *like* a thief."

Problem: The reader recognizes that the statement is not to be taken literally, but does not properly relate the figurative expression with its intended meaning.

Solution: Use the same solutions as given in (2), (3), and (4) under METAPHOR.

📖 Acts 6:15 (NLT) "everyone stared at Stephen because his face became *as bright as* an angel's."

📖 1 Peter 1:24 (LB) "Yes, our natural lives *will fade* as grass does when it becomes brown and dry."

(NLT) "People are like grass *that dies away*."

(CEV) "Humans *wither* like grass."

📖 Revelation 3:3 (NLT) "I will come upon you *suddenly, as unexpected* as a thief."

(CEV) "I will come *when you least expect it*, just as a thief does."

SKEWING BETWEEN GRAMMAR AND SEMANTICS —a lack of correspondence between grammatical word classes (nouns, verbs, adjectives, adverbs, conjunctions) and semantic word classes (things, events, attributes, and relations). Sometimes skewing of word classes is permitted in the source language but may not be permitted in the receptor language. For example, the meaning of a noun that expresses an event idea may need to be re-expressed as a verb.

A word class may be *thing* (water, John, God, father, him), *event* (eat, salvation, chosen), *attribute* (red, small, many, holy), *relation* (and, because, if, therefore), *thing-attribute* (the poor [the poor people], *thing-event* (preacher [a person who preaches], commandment [what someone commands]), or *event-attribute* (sanctification [to make holy]).

Problems:
1. The receptor language does not have an equivalent word of the same grammatical class as a word in the source language. In Greek and English, events may be expressed by *verbs* (save, laugh, speak, walk, see), by *nouns* (salvation, laughter), and by *adjectives* (running, failing). Reference to an event may also be combined with

a reference to a person in *nouns* (savior, preacher). The receptor language may not have a noun that is equivalent to an event noun in the source language.

- Acts 4:12 (NRSV) "There is *salvation* in no one else."
- Romans 13:13 (NRSV) "Let us live honorably as in the day, not in *reveling* and *drunkenness*, not in *debauchery* and *licentiousness*, not in *quarreling* and *jealousy*."
- Ephesians 1:7 (NIV) "In him we have *redemption* through his blood, the *forgiveness* of sins, in accordance with the riches of God's *grace*."
- 2 Peter 2:5 (NIV) "Noah, a *preacher* of righteousness."

Solution: Translate with a verb to express the event and supply the participants involved with the event if needed.

- Acts 4:12 (CEV) "Only Jesus has the power *to save!*"
  (NCV) "Jesus is the only One who *can save people*."
- Romans 13:13 (CEV) "So behave properly, as people do in the day. Don't *go to wild parties* or *get drunk* or *be vulgar* or *indecent. Don't quarrel* or *be jealous*."
- Ephesians 1:7 (CEV) "Christ sacrificed his life's blood *to set us free*, which means that our sins *are* now *forgiven*. Christ did this because God *was so kind* to us."
  (NLT) "He is so rich in kindness that he *purchased our freedom* through the blood of his Son, and our sins *are forgiven*." (Similarly TEV.)
- 2 Peter 2:5 (TEV) "Noah, *who preached* righteousness." (Similarly CEV.)
  (NLT) "Noah *warned the world* of God's righteous judgment."

2. It is difficult to express the meaning of the source text in the receptor language.

Solution: Analyze the source text according to semantic classes and express the text as semantic propositions:
   (a) Find all the event ideas and express them as verbs.
   (b) Fill in the participants of all the events.
   (c) Express the relationships between the propositions.
   (d) Word the translation in a way that will accurately and naturally communicate the same meaning.

SOCIOLINGUISTIC SETTING —the use of language that is appropriate to the social context. For example, there may be a

distinction between formal and informal levels of language, or between literary and technical versus common language. Certain speech may be appropriate for a senior person addressing a junior person, or vice versa. Certain expressions may be used only by a man, or only by a woman.

Problem: The translation has not taken into account the appropriate kind of language the context calls for in relation to the receptor language culture.

Solution: The translator must be aware of these factors and a literary consultant would be very useful for checking the translation.

SOUND SYMBOLISM —the communication of meaning through sound. This includes *ideophones* in which a character or graphic symbol stands for a particular word or phrase, *onomatopoeia* in which words are used whose sound suggest the sense of the word, and *alliteration* in which there is repetition of sounds in two or more words or syllables.

Problem: The translator cannot carry these qualities over into the translation.

Solution: This loss of meaningful word sounds in the translation is to be expected. The meaning of the text must be communicated.

SPEECH QUOTATION —the words spoken by a person. The quotation may take the form of direct or indirect quotation, or, in some languages, semi-direct quotation. Some languages prefer one type of speech quotation and use another type only under specific conditions. For example, one language always uses indirect speech forms except at the climax of a narrative or when the main participant is speaking.

Problem: The target language does not use the same type of quotations as the source language.

Solutions: Study the natural quotation pattern of the receptor language and follow that pattern.

1. Indirect speech may be changed to direct speech.
   📖 Mark 3:9 (TEV) "The crowd was so large that Jesus told his disciples to get a boat ready for him" becomes "The crowd was so large that Jesus said to his disciples, 'Get a boat ready for me.'"

2. Direct speech may be changed to indirect speech.

📖 Mark 1:37 (NRSV) "When they found him, they said to him, 'Everyone is searching for you.'" becomes "When they found him, they told him that everyone was searching for him."

3. A language which uses only the equivalent of "say" instead of the variety of speech verbs found in the Greek text such as, command, promise, beg, rebuke, pray, ask, tell, and proclaim, can indicate the force of the speech act with other words.
   📖 Mark 5:18 (REB) "the man who had been possessed begged to go with him" becomes "the man who had been possessed said, 'Please let me go with you.'"

SYMBOLISM —linguistic forms or cultural actions to which people of a particular culture ascribe a special meaning.
📖 Genesis 24:2 (NIV) "*Put your hand under my thigh*. I want you to swear . . ."
📖 Luke 18:13 (NIV) "He would not even look up to heaven, but *beat his breast*."
📖 Acts 7:54 (NRSV) "they became enraged *and ground their teeth* at Stephen."

Problem: An action in the translation has the same form, but the function is not equivalent to what was intended.

Solutions:
1. When the reader does not understand why the action is done, make the function explicit or explain with a footnote.
   📖 Genesis 24:2 (TEV) "Place your hand between my thighs and make a vow." Footnote: "This was the way in which a vow was made absolutely unchangeable."
   📖 Luke 18:13 (NLT) "Instead, he beat his chest *in sorrow*."
   (CEV) "*He was so sorry for what he had done that* he pounded on his chest."
   📖 Acts 7:54 (TEV) "they became furious and ground their teeth at him *in anger*."

2. If there is already a symbolic meaning attached to it (such as anger, or pride) and making the function explicit results in a conflict of meaning, substitute the function for the action.
   📖 Genesis 24:2 (CEV) "*Solemnly promise* me."
   📖 Luke 18:13 "He would not even look up to heaven, but *was filled with remorse*."
   📖 Acts 7:54 (CEV) "they were angry and *furious*."

3. Use a near equivalent action that already has the correct symbolic meaning in the receptor-language culture.
   - 📖 Luke 18:13 "He would not even look up to heaven, but *hung his head*."
   - 📖 Acts 7:54 (NLT) "they *shook their fists in rage*."

TENSE AND ASPECT —tense indicates the time of an event, whether past, present, or future. Aspect indicates the viewpoint of the speaker with respect to an event: whether the action is completed or incomplete, beginning, continuing, or ending, realis or irrealis (i.e., actual versus imaginary or future), etc. Sometimes a verb may refer to a time or aspect that is different from what is suggested by the surface form (e.g., a present tense verb can, in certain contexts, refer to future times). But this may not be possible or appropriate in the receptor language.
- 📖 Matthew 26:2 (KJV) "Ye know that after two days is the feast of the passover, and the Son of man *is betrayed* to be crucified."
- 📖 John 1:29 (KJV) "The next day John *seeth* Jesus coming unto him."
- 📖 Acts 23:30 (NRSV) "I *sent* him to you at once."
- 📖 Romans 11:9 (NRSV) "And David *says*."
- 📖 1 John 3:9 (NRSV) "Those who have been born of God *do not sin*."

Problem: The tense or aspect indicated by the verb in the source language is not used in the receptor language in the same way.

Solution: Use the tense and aspect that fit the context. In some languages, past tense may carry the story while present tense is used for background information. Other languages may have other patterns in which verb forms must be selected for naturalness.
- 📖 Matthew 26:2 (TEV) "In two days, as you know, it will be the Passover Festival, and the Son of Man *will be handed over* to be crucified." (Similarly CEV, ISV, NCV, NET, NIV, NLT, NRSV, REB.)
- 📖 John 1:29 (NRSV) "The next day he *saw* Jesus coming toward him." (Similarly CEV, ISV, NET, NIV, NLT, NRSV, REB.)
- 📖 Acts 23:30 (TEV) "at once I *decided to send* him to you." (REB) "so I *am sending* him to you without delay." (Similarly ISV.)
- 📖 Romans 11:9 (CEV) "Then David *said*."
- 📖 1 John 3:9 (TEV) "Whoever is a child of God does not *continue to sin*." (Similarly CEV, NCV, NIV.)

TEXTUAL VARIANT —an addition, omission, or alternative reading occurring in another Hebrew or Greek manuscript. The original biblical texts were copied by hand and then, over many centuries, these copies were copied again. Each time a text was copied, a few mistakes might be made. Because of this, there are now many differences among the thousands of existing manuscripts. Scholars have evaluated these differences and have tried to determine which reading most likely represents what the author originally wrote. Many of the variations do not make a significant difference in the meaning. Some do, however, and in these cases the translator has to decide which meaning to translate.

Problems:
1. The translator is puzzled about what the text should be because of textual variants.

   Solution: Follow the text with the best justification. The UBS Greek New Testament shows the important variations of the text and has rated them from A to D to indicate the degree of certainty there was in deciding which to include in the body of the text and which to put in the apparatus. When departing from an A rating, a translator should be able to explain why another text was chosen. It is important to consider how various versions have decided and also when they include a footnote with the alternative reading. If a national version chose a reading that is different from the translation, then a footnote can be added to give the other reading.
   📖 Mark 9:29 (LNT) "Jesus replied, 'This kind can be cast out only by prayer." Footnote: "Some manuscripts add *and fasting*." (Similarly NIV, NRSV, REB.)
   (ISV) "He told them, 'This kind can come out only by prayer and fasting.'" Footnote: "Other mss. lack *and fasting*."
   📖 1 John 1:4 (NIV) "We write this to make our joy complete." Footnote: "Some manuscripts *your*." (Similarly CEV, ISV, NET, NLT, NRSV, TEV.)

2. A verse or passage is not included in the best available manuscripts, but it is included in standard versions used in the national language.
   📖 Mark 16:9-20 and John 8:1-11 are not included in the best available manuscripts but are in the Textus Receptus manuscripts.

   Solution: Include these passages, but identify them as not being part of the original text.

📖 Mark 16:9–20 (NCV). The passage is included in the text within square brackets. There is also information given in the section heading: "Verses 9–20 are not included in two of the best and oldest Greek manuscripts of Mark." (Similarly NET.)

(CEV) The passage is not within square brackets, but has a section heading "One Old Ending to Mark's Gospel" and has a footnote "Verses 9–20 are not in some manuscripts." (Similarly NLT, NRSV, TEV.)

(NIV) The passage is not within square brackets, but has a section heading in square brackets "[The earliest manuscripts and some other ancient witnesses do not have Mark 16:9-20.]"

(REB) The passage is not within square brackets but has a footnote explaining the problem. (Also ISV.)

THEME —the main events in the development of the narrative or statements in the development of an argument. It is in contrast to the material that supports the theme of a unit.

Problem: The reader does not recognize the theme of a unit and consequently does not realize how the narrative or argument is developing. The focus or emphasis that is important to the message is missed.

Solution: The translation needs to use the receptor language discourse features to make the theme prominent, to keep the focus where it should occur, and to emphasize the items that should be emphasized.

UNKNOWN IDEA —an animal, plant, artifact, article of clothing, custom, religious ceremony, or feature of geography of the biblical setting that is unknown to readers of the translation. Various solutions are used by translators in translating unknown terms: use of (1) a more specific term, (2) a more generic term, (3) a descriptive phrase, (4) a cultural substitute, or (5) a loan word borrowed from the national language.

Problem: There are no equivalent words for the things that are unknown ideas, yet these things must be referred to in the translation.

Solutions: Various solutions are possible and several should be considered so as to choose the best solution for a specific context.

1. Consider using a more specific term. Sometimes there is no generic word. At other times, the reader may not relate the generic word to the specific word intended unless it is made explicit.
   - 📖 Mark 2:23 (NIV) "they began to pick some heads of *grain*" could be translated (TEV) "they began to pick the heads of *wheat*." (Similarly CEV, NLT.)
   - 📖 Acts 4:20 (NRSV) "we cannot keep from speaking about *what* we have seen and heard" could be translated "we cannot stop telling about *the wonderful things* we saw *Jesus do* and heard *him say*." (Similarly NLT.)

2. Consider using a more generic term.
   - 📖 Matthew 6:28 *flowers* for "lilies." (Also NET.)
   - 📖 Mark 15:13 *kill him* for "crucify him."
   - 📖 Mark 15:39 *officer* for "centurion."
   - 📖 Acts 27:29 *hooks* for "anchors."

3. Consider using a descriptive phrase.
   a. Use a generic term and add specifying components.
      - 📖 Matthew 6:28 *wild flowers* for "lilies." (Also CEV, TEV.)
      - 📖 Matthew 11:19 *a man who eats too much* for "glutton."
      - 📖 Matthew 17:4 *a little house made from branches* for "tabernacle."
      - 📖 Mark 15:13 *nail him to a cross* for "crucify him."
      - 📖 Mark 15:39 *army officer* (so NCV, TEV), or *Roman officer* (so NLT), or *Roman army officer* (so CEV) for "centurion."
      - 📖 John 10:12 *a fierce wild animal* for "wolf."
      - 📖 Acts 27:29 *big iron hooks* for "anchors."
   b. Use a generic term and add a description of the function.
      - 📖 Matthew 23:22 *the chair where God sits to rule* for "the throne of God."
      - 📖 John 10:12 *an animal that kills sheep* for "wolf."
      - 📖 Acts 27:29 *hooks that stop the boat* for "anchors."
      - 📖 Acts 27:40 *a board used to steer the boat* for "rudder."
   c. Use a generic term and add descriptions of both form and function.
      - 📖 Matthew 12:9 the *Jewish meeting place* (so CEV) for synagogue

UNKNOWN IDEA

- 📖 Mark 15:13 *kill him by nailing him to a cross* for "crucify him."
- 📖 John 10:12 *a wild animal that kills sheep* for "wolf."
- 📖 Acts 27:29 *big iron hooks that stop the boat* for "anchors."

4. Consider using a cultural substitute. A cultural substitute is the use of a different item in a translation for an object or event in the source language that is unknown to the readers, or, if known, its intended function is misunderstood. The substitute should have the same function in context, be as similar in form as possible, and be compatible with biblical culture. Cultural substitutes should not be used if they conflict with historical facts. There are times when cultural substitutes may be useful in non-historical material. If retaining the historical culture in a didactic passage or a figure of speech results in obscurity or causes the translation to become complicated and wordy, the cultural substitute can be a good solution. Units of measurement and weight may be expressed in terms used in the receptor language.
   - 📖 Matthew 26:20 (KJV) "he *sat down* [instead of *reclined*] with the twelve."
   - 📖 John 21:8 (NIV) "for they were not far from the shore, about *a hundred yards* [instead of *two hundred cubits*]." (Similarly CEV, ISV, NCV, NET, NRSV, REB, TEV.)
   (NLT) "for they were only out about *three hundred feet*."
   - 📖 1 Peter 5:8 "Your adversary the devil prowls around like a roaring *leopard* [instead of *lion*]."

5. Consider using a loan word. This is a word borrowed from the national language or another known language for use in the translation. It is a foreign word to the readers of the translation and thus different from other national language words that have already been assimilated into the normal vocabulary of the receptor language.

   Problem: An unknown concept is translated by a loan word and most of the readers do not know the meaning of the loan word.

   Solutions: The loan words in the suggestions are transliterations of Greek words so as to bring out the foreign quality presented by this solution.

   1. Names of people, places, and events with no equivalent in the receptor language can best be translated with loan

UNKNOWN IDEA   81

words. A generic classifier may accompany names of places where this is helpful. People: Iesous, Kornelios, Zebedaios; Places: *city of* Hierosoluma, *land of* Galilaia, Iordanes *River.*

2. A few other words seem to be most easily translated with loan words accompanied by descriptive words or phrases where important historical facts are involved.
   - 📖 Mark 1:6 "John wore clothing made from the hair of *a large animal called kamelos.*"
   - 📖 Mark 14:1 "After two days was *the festival called Pascha.*"
   (KJV) "After two days was *the feast of the passover.*"
   (NLT) "It was now two days before *the Passover celebration.*"
   - 📖 Mark 15:23 "They offered Jesus wine mixed with *a drug called smurna.*"
   (TEV) "There they tried to give him wine mixed with *a drug called myrrh.*"
   (NLT) "They offered him wine *drugged with myrrh.*"
   (Similarly REB.)

3. For most other cases, loan words do not help communicate the meaning and another solution should be sought.

VOCATIVE —a term of address, indicating the relationship between the speaker and the person or people to whom he is speaking.

Problems:
1. The words used in the vocative may imply a different relationship than the original.
   - 📖 John 2:4 (NASB) "And Jesus said to her, '*Woman*, what does that have to do with us?'"

   Solution: Use a word that matches the intention of the original.
   - 📖 John 2:4 (NIV) "'*Dear woman*, why do you involve me?' Jesus replied." (Similarly NCV.)
   - 📖 John 2:4 (CEV) "Jesus replied, '*Mother*, my time hasn't yet come!'"
   (REB) "He answered, 'That is no concern of mine.'" (Similarly NLT.)
   (TEV) "'You must not tell me what to do,' Jesus replied."

2. The vocative must come first in the sentence in many languages, but in the source language it often comes imbedded in a sentence.
   - Psalm 108:5 (NLT) "Be exalted, Oh God, above the highest heavens."
   - Luke 5:8 (KJV) "Depart from me; for I sinful man, O Lord."

   Solution: Begin the sentence with the vocative when this is the preferred pattern in the language.
   - Psalm 108:5 (REB) "God, be exalted above the heavens."
   - Luke 5:8 (CEV) "Lord, don't come near me! I am a sinner." (Similarly NLT.)

ZEUGMA
—one word is used to modify or govern two or more words so that it applies to each in a different sense or it properly collocates with only one of the words.
- 1 Cor. 3:2 "I gave you milk *to drink*, not solid food."
- 1 Tim. 4:3 "*forbidding* to marry, to abstain from foods."
- Rev. 11:1 (NRSV) "Come and *measure* the temple of God and the altar and those who worship there."

Problem: The same verb does not collocate with both objects.

Solutions:
1. Use different verbs that collocate correctly.
   - 1 Tim. 4:3 (NRSV) "They *forbid* marriage and *demand* abstinence from food." (Similarly KJV, NCV, NIV, REB.)
     (CEV) "will forbid people to marry or to eat certain foods." (Similarly ISV.)
     (NLT) "They will say it is wrong to be married and wrong to eat certain foods."
   - Rev. 11:1 (TEV) "Go and *measure* the temple of God and the altar, and *count* those who are worshipping in the temple." (Similarly ISV, NCV, NIV, NLT, REB.)

2. Use a generic verb.
   - 1 Cor. 3:2 (NRSV) "I *fed* you with milk, not solid food." (Similarly NLT, REB.)
     (NIV) "I gave you milk, not solid food." (Similarly ISV, NCV.)

SYSTEMATIC RECORDING OF CONSULTANT NOTES

The Summer Institute of Linguistics has developed a systematic way of recording consultant notes and information from other sources that is relevant to a particular verse or passage. This system is called CONNOT (Consultant Notes) and is now being used extensively. It makes it possible to build a database of information on translation issues that have arisen in different languages, including exegetical studies and good renderings. Users can readily access all notes relevant to a particular verse or passage. They can also access all notes on a particular kind of translation issue.

Translation consultants can use the CONNOT system at various stages in checking translations. CONNOT notes are mainly used in two ways:
1. They are used by consultants for checking translations with a translation team. Some consultants make notes before the translation session, working from a back-translation. They identify points for discussion and send these notes to the translation team in advance of the session. The team may also send responses on some of these points back to the consultant before the session. Other consultants make notes after the checking session, recording good renderings to share with other teams or noting significant issues that have been discussed or which need further discussion.
2. Notes may also be built up into a database. Many consultants find it helpful to build their own personal database on each Bible book, so that they can pull this up when checking the same book with another team. Over time, a rich resource of exegetical notes and suggested renderings can be compiled. Some entities may choose to develop their own database, combining notes from branch consultants. There is potential for building databases in major languages, such as French, Spanish, and Portuguese.

Notes that are likely to be widely useful to translation teams are being built into a general database by the SIL International Translation Department in Dallas. This database is currently referred to as the CONNOT database. It is being made available on the Translator's Workplace CD-ROM. Notes on specific books can be requested on diskette or by e-mail.

Each note (called a **record**) is composed of several **fields**, one field for each kind of information. Each field begins with a backslash and three-letter lowercase code to designate the field. Following the code, there should be one space and then the specific information filled in.

Here is the full list of standard format markers for the fields. They are listed in the order in which they should be entered in a record. Of all the possible fields, the only obligatory fields are \ref and \dis. Other fields are used as they are pertinent. There should not be more than one of a given field marker in a record.

\ref **reference**. This gives the book, chapter and verse reference of the verse or passage. Spell out the names of the books in full (Revelation, not Rev). Use Arabic numerals with book names (3 John, not III John). According to your preference, separate chapter and verse numbers with either a colon or a period (John 3:16 or John 3.16). For a reference to a passage of two or more verses, join the beginning and ending numbers with a hyphen (Mark 4:1-2, not Mark 4:1, 2 and not Mark 4:1ff).

For a note on a footnote, give the verse reference for which the footnote applies and specify the footnote category in the \cat field. For a section heading, give the range of the passage for the whole section and specify the section heading category in the \cat field. For reference to a whole chapter, give the range of the first verse to the last verse of the chapter. For reference to a whole book, give only the book name without chapters and verses.
Examples:
   \ref Mark 2:12
   \ref 2 Corinthians 1:2-3
   \ref Exodus 20:1-26
   \ref 1 Peter

\txt **text**. This is a quotation from the text of a fairly literal version and should be present for all records that discuss a specific verse, a part of a verse, connected parts of a range of verses, or a section heading. Omit this field for records discussing a range of verses in general or the entire book.

Begin with the three- or four-letter abbreviation of the version in capitals (NASB, NET, RSV, or NIV). After a single space, quote only the part of the verse that is being discussed, without quotation marks except where they appear within the quoted version. Do not add ellipsis marks at the beginning or the end of the part quoted even if it is less than an entire verse. Ellipsis marks are used only if text is omitted from within the part quoted.

If it is helpful to quote the text from more than one version, start each subsequent version on a new line with the abbreviation of the version without repeating the \txt field code. When quoting from Today's English Version (Good News Bible), use the abbreviation TEV, not GNB. When the text is that of a section heading, the words "section heading" should follow the version abbreviation.
Examples:
 \txt NASB When the Counselor comes . . . he will testify about me.
 TEV The Helper will come . . . and he will speak about me.
 \txt NIV section heading The Supremacy of Christ

\ren **rendering**. This is a back-translation of the receptor language translation. In order to be of use in the general CONNOT database, give this in English. If the original was in French or Spanish, it should be translated into English. It is possible to include the French or Spanish back-translation in a separate field just before the \ren field with the field designation \renf or \rens.

\cat **category**. This is the specific category of the translation problem involved in the discussion. There is a limited set of category labels: those presented in this book. The use of this field is optional, but a category label is included for each record in the general CONNOT database.

The category label should be given with the first letter capitalized and the rest of the category label in lowercase letters (Tense and aspect, not Tense and Aspect). For categories that have subcategories (lettered a, b, etc.), the main category title should be followed by a colon, single space, and the subcategory (which should begin with a lowercase letter). "Key biblical term" should always be followed with a colon, single space, and the key term being discussed. The category name (with a subcategory or key term) should be followed by a single space and, in brackets, the one- or two-letter abbreviation designating that category group.
Examples:
 \cat Interpretation of source text [E]
 \cat Lexical correspondence: consistency [L]
 \cat Key biblical term: angel [L]

If there are separate discussions about two or more categories in the same verse, each discussion should have its own complete record. However, if multiple categories are interrelated and handled in the same discussion, the various category labels

should be listed one after another, separated by commas, all following the single \cat field marker. Example:
 \cat Genre [D], Cross-cultural mismatch [Cu]

\dis **discussion.** This is a discussion of the exegetical or translation point that prompted recording this note. It should explain the factors that need to be considered. It might include suggestions for alternative renderings. If this discussion is given to point out a good example of how it can be translated in the \ren field, the comment "Good rendering" should be added at the beginning of the discussion.

For transliterated Greek, use e~ for eta and o~ for omega. New paragraphs within the discussion should start on a new line (i.e., preceded by a return <Enter>) but should not be indented. A blank line may be left between paragraphs.

\sug **suggestion.** In this field should go any suggested alternative renderings that the consultant offers the translation team to consider. Content other than suggested renderings should be put in the \dis field.

\res **response.** In this field should go the response and action taken by the translation team to questions and suggestions given in the discussion field. This field is especially useful when the consultant and translation team are exchanging preliminary notes in writing before the face-to-face check. It is used only in interaction between a consultant and a translation team and is not included in the general CONNOT database.

\tst **testing question.** This is a question that the translation team should ask mother-tongue speakers of the receptor language in order to see whether the translation adequately communicates the meaning. An explanation may be included to alert the translation team as to the purpose of the question.

Although there is usually a \dis field in each record, occasionally it may be convenient to have only a \tst field without a \dis field. In such cases, the category label should be "Testing question."

\mem **memo.** This is where notes can be added that are only intended for the consultant's own database. It is used only in interaction between a consultant and a translation team and is not included in the general CONNOT database.

\lng **language name.** This is the name of the receptor language, the language into which the translation is made. If possible include the language family and the country in parentheses. Example:
 \lng Otomi (Otomanguean, Mexico)

\src   **source.** This is the name of the consultant who recorded the note or the reference to a book or article from which a quotation is taken.
Examples:
\src John Smith
\src Stott, John. *Romans: God's Good News for the World.* Downers Grove, Ill.: InterVarsity Press, 1994. pp. 47–50.

\dat   **date.** This is the date on which the note was made (mm/yy, or yyyy if the month is not known). Examples:
\dat 5/99
\dat 1984

Contributions of notes for the database are warmly welcomed. These may be a note on an interesting point that arose in a translation or checking session, a good rendering of a difficult verse, a summary note resulting from exegetical research on a problem passage, or a helpful extract from a commentary or other reference source (include full bibliographical information please). If possible, send notes for the general CONNOT database by e-mail or on diskette. When sending notes by e-mail, address them to Translators_Workplace@sil.org and put the word CONNOT somewhere in the subject line.

www.ingramcontent.com/pod-product-compliance
Lightning Source LLC
Chambersburg PA
CBHW051816230426
43672CB00012B/2751